Praise for

Ecothrifty

I support & endorse this wonderful book, 100%.

—Ed Begley, Jr. Actor / Environmentalist

If you care about the future of the Earth and her ecosystems
and want to make a difference, pick up a copy of this book and
read it cover to cover. You're in for a treat! This book is chock-full
of valuable information that could change your lifestyle and help
create a sustainable world. Ecothrifty should be required
reading for every citizen of the world.

—Dan Chiras, Director, The Evergreen Institute, and author of
The Homeowner's Guide to Renewable Energy, and *Power from the Sun*
evergreeninstitute.org

Those of us embarking on the journey of consuming less
and enjoying ourselves more desperately need guidebooks, and
Deborah Niemann has written one for us. *Ecothrifty* leads us gently
down the path of changing the way we think about what we buy.
I hope you will find this book the beginning of your engagement
in a global movement to create a family life that is rich and
abundant while sitting lighter on the planet that holds us all.

—Kathy Harrison, from the Foreword

ECO
THRIFTY

Cheaper, Greener Choices
for a Happier, Healthier Life

DEBORAH NIEMANN

new society
PUBLISHERS

Cover design by Diane McIntosh.
Cover image © iStock.

Printed in Canada. First printing August 2012.

Paperback ISBN: 978-0-86571-715-2
Ebook ISBN: 978-1-55092-510-4

Inquiries regarding requests to reprint all or part of *Ecothrifty*
should be addressed to New Society Publishers at the address below.

To order directly from the publishers, please call toll-free (North America)
1-800-567-6772, or order online at www.newsociety.com

Any other inquiries can be directed by mail to:

New Society Publishers
P.O. Box 189, Gabriola Island, BC V0R 1X0, Canada
(250) 247-9737

New Society Publishers' mission is to publish books that contribute in fundamental ways
to building an ecologically sustainable and just society, and to do so with the least possible
impact on the environment, in a manner that models this vision. We are committed to doing
this not just through education, but through action. The interior pages of our bound books
are printed on Forest Stewardship Council®-registered acid-free paper that is **100% post-
consumer recycled** (100% old growth forest-free), processed chlorine free, and printed
with vegetable-based, low-VOC inks, with covers produced using FSC®-registered stock.
New Society also works to reduce its carbon footprint, and purchases carbon offsets based
on an annual audit to ensure a carbon neutral footprint. For further information, or to browse
our full list of books and purchase securely, visit our website at: **www.newsociety.com**

Library and Archives Canada Cataloguing in Publication

Niemann, Deborah
     Ecothrifty : cheaper, greener choices for a happier, healthier life /
     Deborah Niemann.

Includes bibliographical references and indexes.
ISBN 978-0-86571-715-2

     1. Sustainable living--Economic aspects. 2. Thriftiness--Environmental
     aspects. 3. Consumer education. 4. Health. 5. Happiness. I. Title.

GE196.N53 2012   640   C2012-905690-1

For
my children
It's your turn now!

Books for Wiser Living
recommended by *Mother Earth News*

Today, more than ever before, our society is seeking ways to live more conscientiously. To help bring you the very best inspiration and information about greener, more sustainable lifestyles, *Mother Earth News* is recommending select New Society Publishers books to its readers. For more than 30 years, *Mother Earth* has been North America's "Original Guide to Living Wisely," creating books and magazines for people with a passion for self-reliance and a desire to live in harmony with nature. Across the countryside and in our cities, New Society Publishers and *Mother Earth* are leading the way to a wiser, more sustainable world. For more information, please visit MotherEarthNews.com

Contents

Acknowledgments

Like any book ever written, this one required the vision and assistance of many people. Many thanks to the editorial team at New Society Publishers for bringing this book to fruition, and especially to my editor Janice Logan.

Thank you to everyone who took the time to tell me about your hobbies, your green passions, and your lives. I learned a lot from all of you who agreed to share your stories within the pages of this book.

I am also eternally grateful to my children. The not-so-simple decision to become a mother changed the trajectory of my life. Because I wanted you to have a healthier and happier childhood than I did, I started reading and researching. Without you, I would not have questioned the standard American diet or common practices in modern medicine. Had I not become a mom, I never would have had the knowledge to write this book. And my husband deserves a huge thank you for always being willing to try something new whenever I suggested yet another change to our diet or lifestyle.

Foreword

By Kathy Harrison

I'm old enough to have lived through six decades of system shocks. I remember the oil embargo in the early seventies. We could buy gas only on odd or even days, depending on the last number on our license plate and we were restricted to four dollars' worth although, granted, four dollars bought a lot more gas then than it does now. I remember turning down the heat and putting on a sweater and feeling mighty virtuous in the process. This was a decade of social unrest fueled by the Vietnam War and the battle for civil rights for woman and blacks. I witnessed urban warfare in Watts and unarmed students die at Kent State. Fueled by our distrust of the system and a desire to live a life that was simpler and lived closer to the land, my husband, Bruce, and I took our young son and joined a small army of young people opting out of the rat race, seeking peace in the country.

We moved to a small farm in the hills of Western Massachusetts, bought a cow and a flock of chickens and put in a huge garden. We learned the intricacies of cooking on a one hundred year-old wood-fired kitchen range and put up our first batch of maple syrup. They were good years. Our children thrived and we put down roots, deep and persistent.

Fast forward forty years. We lived through the years of leisure suits (really!) and big hair. Dot com bubbles, parachute pants and bands we can no longer remember the names of came and went. McMansions flourished and decades of a consumption-fueled frenzy defined who we were. The shocks continued. We saw the Twin Towers fall in Technicolor on our big-screen televisions. Katrina gave us some first-hand experience with who wins in a battle between man and nature. The Gulf of Mexico was fouled by the Deep Water oil spill. Massive earthquakes and out-of-control wild fires dominated the evening news. Failing economies, ineffective governmental response to crisis and melting polar ice became the new normal.

Through it all, many of us figured some things out. Big isn't always better. Sometimes big is a lot worse and real change seldom occurs at the macro level. The good things happening in the world are micro in scope and not often the stuff of headlines. And there is a lot of good stuff. There are community gardens and food preservation cooperatives. There are local transition initiatives and seed lending libraries. Food buying groups and CSA's are supplying families with affordable, local, organic food. People have stopped waiting for governments to respond to the twin threats of financial collapse and climate change catastrophe. Some of us (and more every day) have decided to take the futures of our families and our environment into our own hands. We have stopped thinking about recycling in isolation. Making a difference in the waste stream also means buying less. Getting a handle on our personal finances is within our reach where controlling municipal debt is often beyond our control.

Those of us embarking on the journey of consuming less and enjoying ourselves more desperately need guidebooks. Deborah Niemann has written one for us. *Ecothrifty* leads us gently down the path of changing the way we think about what we buy. I have been living a frugal lifestyle for forty years and I still found myself taking notes, dog-earing pages and leaving each page inspired and energized. Many people share a concern about the future of our planet and I believe worry over our economic future is nearly universal. Still, it's difficult to find true, doable solutions and unique ideas for a personal response. The push to encourage us to spend money to buy happiness is ongoing and advertisers know exactly what they're doing. They target us and, and they especially target our children with bigger, better, more enticing products. But products are not food. Products don't nourish us or make us prettier or happier or healthier. Products hold the seeds of our destruction. We need books that shed a light on this not just for ourselves but for our children and for their children. I hope you will find this book the beginning of your engagement in a global movement to create a family life that is rich and abundant while sitting lighter on the planet that holds us all.

Kathy Harrison is a writer, teacher and small scale farmer. She and her family raise bees, vegetables and poultry on Barefoot Farm in the hills of Western Massachusetts. Kathy teaches food preservation classes at a variety of venues including NOFA and Greenfield Community College. She is the author of several books, including *Just In Case: How To Be Self-Sufficient When the Unexpected Happens*. She also writes for Lehman's Non-Electric Catalog's County Life blog series.

You can see more of her writing at www.justincasebook.wordpress. com and www.preservingabundance.com.

Introduction

"I'd buy organic food if it weren't so expensive." "I'd buy compact fluorescent bulbs if they cost the same as regular light bulbs." "I'd buy a hybrid car if it cost the same as other cars." If any of these statements could be yours, you are not alone. But you are misinformed. Sadly, many people think that making the green choice is making the more expensive choice. Although this can be true, it doesn't have to be. Yes, it costs more to buy an organic frozen dinner than it does to buy one that contains conventionally grown and, often, artificial ingredients. But the ecothrifty choice is the one that saves money and is better for the environment. The ecothrifty choice for dinner is one that is cooked from scratch. An organic frozen dinner is not environmentally friendly with its two or three layers of packaging, some of which are not even recyclable or biodegradable.

"But I don't have time to cook!" "I don't know how to cook." "After working a hard day, I shouldn't have to come home and cook." Madison Avenue marketing executives and advertisers have driven home the ideas that cooking is difficult and time consuming and no one should have to do it and that we are all entitled to eat whatever we want, whenever we want it, without having to do anything other than hand over a few dollars. Television shows like *Top Chef* have turned cooking into a spectator sport, and how can the average person compete with that? Gone are

1

the days of Julia Child telling everyone that they can cook. How much is your time worth? For most of us, time at home is worth exactly zero dollars because no one is paying us when we are not at the office. Since I'm a freelance writer, the more time I spend at my computer, the more I get paid, but I can't spend every waking hour at the computer. As it is, I already spend too much time there, and my body rebels with all sorts of aches and pains. I need to get up, go outside, walk around, and lift stuff. I can join a health club and pay someone else for the privilege of moving my muscles and sweating in their space, or I can garden, take care of animals, cook from scratch, and do things that actually pay me indirectly in terms of money saved and health improved.

I have been running the numbers for years, and although some things may not make a big impact on my bottom line, I'm usually excited about how much money I'm "making" by doing things myself rather than buying them, especially when I am substituting for high-priced items. If I were to buy the raspberries that I use in my raspberry crisp, it would cost $20! And if I bought that whole dessert from a bakery, they'd probably charge at least $40 because they need to make a profit, but honestly, I've never seen a dessert like my crisp for sale because raspberries are just too expensive. No one would put six cups of raspberries in a dessert because they know they wouldn't be able to sell it and make a profit. And my raspberry crisp is made completely from organic ingredients and with very little added sugar, which not all bakeries do. To me, this is priceless.

I could list lots of activities where your time winds up being "worth" $30 or more an hour, which is a good rate for time that otherwise would not pay you a cent. How much are you paid to surf the web, watch television, or play video games? When something is being sold for less than it would cost me to do myself, there often is a very unpleasant reality behind the product price — factory farms, sweat shops in third world countries, illegal immigrants being exploited, or products of such poor quality that they wind up in landfills far too soon. Our cheap food and our cheap stuff are not really cheap at all.

Cooking and food are not the only examples of our giving control to big corporations to take care of us. Gradually we are letting go of all sorts of simple skills. We don't do the math to conclude that a compact fluorescent light bulb will save us money in the long run. We won't consider giving up the heated leather seats to buy the hybrid car at the same price. We continue driving to work instead of using mass transportation or living close enough to walk or bike. In today's world, no one needs to be inconvenienced or to know how to do anything — except spend. You can buy anything you need or want, and you can use all your free time pursuing leisure activities and watching television, where you are exposed to more advertisements encouraging you to want more and buy more.

When advertisers tell us what we want to hear, we believe them without question. It is a well-known phenomenon that communication scholars call confirmation bias. When you believe that your time is too valuable to cook, you will believe that eating out is a good deal financially when an advertisement tells you it is. Conversely, if you really like eating fast food, you will ignore everything negative that you hear about it.

Throughout history, cultures have focused on the attainment of wealth. For individuals and countries, the goal has been to have more land, more money, and more power. And in the past hundred years, we can add corporations to the equation. Just as countries conquered and annexed smaller countries two hundred years ago, big corporations take over smaller or weaker corporations today, creating bigger and more powerful corporations. And we are all helping them by buying their products, whether we need them or not. In many cases, buying one product creates a problem, which then can be solved by buying another product. Making poor nutritional choices often leads to medical conditions such as high blood pressure and diabetes. Although physicians are clear that dietary changes can reverse these conditions, many people would rather continue to eat poorly and take costly medication, which may cause side effects, such as impotence, which will be solved by taking yet another medication.

We really want to believe we can have it all. We can avoid cooking, eat junk food, and stay healthy. We also want to eat fresh tomatoes, bananas, avocados, peaches, and every other imaginable fruit and vegetable twelve months a year, and we want it all for a cheap price, even if the food has to travel three thousand miles or more to get to our plates. We don't want to do physical labor, but we do want to drive ten miles to the gym, where we will spend thirty minutes walking to nowhere on an electric treadmill. We want cosmetics that keep us looking young without giving us cancer. We want a clean house without actually having to clean it. While we complain that we don't have any time, we are watching television somewhere between almost three hours[1] and five hours per day.[2] We ignore the fact that it takes more time to get in the car, drive to a restaurant, wait to be seated, wait for food to be served, and drive home than it would take for us to cook and clean up in our own kitchens. We complain that we don't have enough money to eat healthily, but we are spending less of our incomes on food than at any time in our history. Americans spent 42.5 percent of their incomes on food in 1901, almost 30 percent in 1950, and only 13 percent by 2003, and 42 percent of the money we spend on food is spent away from home.[3]

But according to a growing number of researchers, the party is ending. We are suffering from unprecedented levels of obesity, cancer, high blood pressure, heart disease, depression, and other maladies. Landfills are full, and no one wants a new one in their backyard. Our financial systems are crumbling, from the biggest corporations to average families. Some say food prices will double or triple in the next few years. As the price of oil skyrockets, the price of everything else will follow because if you bought it, a truck brought it. And in our increasingly global economy, the majority of the things we buy were brought to this continent by a ship. Our modern food system is dependent on diesel fuel to run tractors and combines. Fertilizers and pesticides are petroleum based. Plastic packaging is manufactured from petroleum. Cheap appliances now built in Asia require transportation to North America where we purchase them.

Are we doomed? No. There is a lot we can do to save money, conserve our resources, and live a healthier lifestyle. In my first book, *Homegrown and Handmade*,[4] I wrote about how you can grow your own food and fiber, and while those activities certainly help you live a more ecothrifty life, they are pretty big projects. There are many little things you can do on a daily basis to improve your life and protect our environment. One thing you can do — over and over again — is to simply start questioning things that you have always assumed to be true. Maybe your time is not too valuable to cook dinner. Do you really always need to buy new clothes rather than used? Does your child really need the latest plastic gadget from China? Maybe you wouldn't mind drying a few things on a clothesline rather than in a dryer. Could better time management help you save money by avoiding impulse purchases when you are in a hurry?

The most important thing we need to do is to stop making excuses for ourselves to overeat and overspend on things we don't need. This can be hard to hear, and it is the opposite of what marketers have been telling us for decades. When my children were young, I remember spending $40 on paper products — tablecloth, napkins, plates, and decorations — that were thrown away after being used once for my son's birthday party. A tiny voice in my head at the time questioned what I was doing, but the Navy officer's wife in my head wanted to keep up appearances. What would have been the consequence of not buying those items? Nothing negative. I would have saved $40, and a big bag of garbage would have been kept out of the landfill.

The brain always supplies us with excuses when we do something that makes us think twice. In the case of the birthday party, I was an officer's wife, so I thought I had to do things a certain way. Other excuses might include a lack of time or support because you work long hours or are a single parent. Situations like these certainly present challenges, but they can often be overcome. Henry Ford said, "Whether you think you can or you can't, you're right!" Everyone has his or her own personal set of challenges. To overcome your challenges you have to think beyond the marketing ads. As long as you let Madison Avenue tell you how to spend your money and your time, you're a pawn in the marketing game, making others richer. The good news is that you can stop playing that game whenever you are ready.

Are you ready to save money, get healthier, and stop sending so much trash to the landfill? Don't worry — you don't have to move to the middle of nowhere. You can get started wherever you are living. This book offers suggestions for living an ecothrifty life, but this book is only the beginning. Once you start thinking about what you do in your daily life, you will undoubtedly come up with many more ideas that will work for you. Don't worry if you can't implement all of the ideas. Picture this book as a giant intellectual buffet. Take what looks good to you and leave the rest. The important thing simply is to get started. As the saying goes, "A trip of a thousand miles begins with a single step." Are you ready to take that first step?

CHAPTER 1

Personal Care Products

The beauty industry, which has been around for less than a hundred years, is one of the most profitable industries on the planet. Americans alone spend $50 billion a year on skin care and makeup. If you ever thought you might be overpaying for cosmetics and skin care products, you were probably right.

Although many Americans believe that the United States Food and Drug Administration (FDA) verifies the safety of all cosmetics, this is not the case. Unlike drugs, which require approval by the FDA before being marketed, cosmetics require no government approval. The estimate of the number of chemicals used in cosmetics today varies from six thousand to tens of thousands, depending on who is counting. The smaller estimates come from industry groups, whereas the larger numbers come from consumer groups.

The Cosmetic Ingredient Review was created thirty-six years ago to "review and assess the safety of ingredients used in cosmetics." As of August 2011, however, they had reviewed only 2,300 of the 6,000 cosmetic ingredients voluntarily registered with the FDA.[5] The FDA has banned the use of fourteen chemicals in cosmetics.[6] Even if there are only six thousand chemicals used in cosmetics, it is more than enough to make some of us more than a wee bit concerned about safety.

Looking beyond safety, however, how do consumers know that a product does what it claims to do, such as fade age spots or eliminate wrinkles? Does a $330 per ounce eye cream hydrate and nourish skin better than something like olive oil? No one really knows.

What can you do if you don't have an unlimited amount of time to research every ingredient in the personal care and beauty products you use? You can use natural products that have been used safely for hundreds of years without negative side effects. While it is true that natural does not always mean safe, the advantage in using age-old treatments is that the knowledge of their safety — or not — has been passed down for generations. Proponents of chemicals might use poison ivy or arsenic as examples of natural products that are not safe. However, because they have been around forever, everyone knows that they are not safe. Natural products with cosmetic uses, such as baking soda, vinegar, and oatmeal, have been around far longer than modern chemicals. If they were toxic, it would be common knowledge. In contrast, modern scientists have been known to take a dangerous natural substance, such as botulinum, alter it for use as a commercial product and then insist it is safe after only a few years of study.

Making your own skin care products or simply using common ingredients found in most kitchens can save you hundreds or even thousands of dollars a year and ensure you have a non-toxic, safe personal care product vetted by hundreds of years of use. Although I can't guarantee you'll have visibly improved skin in thirty days, I can guarantee that you will save a lot of money, and you won't have to worry about getting cancer in twenty years from using these ingredients daily.

Basics

It is not difficult to make your own body care products. In fact, a single ingredient works well for many purposes. You may need to do a bit of research, and you may not get the ingredient that suits you best the first time you try, but don't give up. It is sad to see people give up on natural products when the first try doesn't live up to expectations. Just as every commercial product is not right for your skin or hair, every natural product is not right for you.

Oils, waxes, and butters are the base ingredients of homemade soaps, creams, lotions, and moisturizers. Household basics like sugar, salt, and baking soda are also used to make safe and effective products.

Oils

Although all of the oils used in ecothrifty personal care products are food oils — not petroleum based — every oil sold in the grocery store is not necessarily good for your skin. Each oil has a different acid composition, giving it unique properties. Some are more moisturizing; others work better in soaps. Most of the popular cooking oils, such as canola, corn, cottonseed, and soy, should be avoided because they are not particularly good for your skin, and unless you are buying organic products, they come from genetically modified (GM) crops, which are heavily sprayed with herbicides. Also avoid "vegetable oil" because it is usually some combination of these oils. The skin is the largest organ of the body and does an excellent job of absorbing into the bloodstream whatever is rubbed on it. Some systemic drugs are even administered through a skin patch now.

The following list of oils is not anywhere close to complete. It includes a few of the more commonly used oils that are also fairly easy to find and purchase. If you can't find them locally, they are available through a number of online retailers. Most are not very expensive, so buy small quantities of several and see which ones your skin prefers. Any oils that you decide you don't like for body care products can usually be used in cooking.

- **Apricot kernel oil** — This oil is considered excellent for your skin. It has a lighter feel than many oils and is easily absorbed into your skin, making it a great choice for moisturizing. But apricot oil makes a softer bar of soap, so use it sparingly in soap recipes. It also works well as massage oil and in salt and sugar scrubs. Be sure to buy only what you plan to use within six months to a year because apricot kernel oil tends to go rancid more quickly than other oils, although storing it in the refrigerator will slow down the aging process a bit.

- **Castor oil** — Used therapeutically for centuries, a small amount of castor oil is found in quite a few soap recipes. It is also popular for adding to butters when making lip balm. Its reputed benefits are far too numerous to be listed here, but if you have any skin conditions, you might want to research this oil further. It is good for dry or damaged skin, but it does not make good massage oil because it is thick and sticky.

- **Coconut oil** — If you are going to make your own soap, you will find that almost every recipe includes coconut oil because it creates great lather. Most people don't believe soap is doing anything if they don't see suds, which is why coconut oil is such a popular soap ingredient. Although it is possible to make soap without coconut oil, be aware that the soap may not be sudsy. Coconut oil is a great choice for making laundry soap because it is so good at cleaning. However, it can be quite drying, so bar soap is not usually made with only coconut oil. And multitasking coconut oil also makes tasty popcorn, flaky pie crusts, and soft tortillas.

- **Grape seed oil** — If you want a product that people say has miraculous properties, grape seed oil is worth a try. It is reputed to have regenerative qualities like the commercial creams costing a hundred dollars an ounce or more, but you can buy grape seed oil for far less than a dollar per ounce. It makes excellent massage oil as it is thin and very slippery, and it makes a great addition to sugar or salt scrubs.

- **Olive oil** — Olive oil is great for your skin, so it is usually a good choice to use as a moisturizer, either alone or in combination with other oils. It is also a good choice for using in soaps, although most people today do not like to use 100 percent olive oil because it will not make a very hard bar of soap. This means it will be used up quickly, especially if you do not keep it in a soap dish that allows for complete drainage of water.

- **Palm kernel oil** — This oil comes from a different part of the palm tree than palm oil, and it has different properties. It creates more lather and a harder bar than palm oil when used in making soap, but it can be drying if used as the predominant oil in a soap recipe.

Unfortunately, a lot of palm kernel oil and palm oil today comes from areas that have been deforested to create palm plantations. These areas happen to be the natural habitat of orangutans, a species in danger of extinction as a result of loss of habitat. As of this writing, I have not seen any sustainable palm kernel oil on the market, so I have quit using it for the time being.

- **Palm oil** — Palm oil creates suds when used in soap recipes. Many expensive soaps list sodium palmate and/or sodium cocoate as ingredients. These terms refer to palm oil and coconut oil saponified with sodium hydroxide, also known as lye. Coconut oil and palm oil are inexpensive compared to other oils used in soap making, which is why they are usually the predominant oils in commercial soaps, including expensive soaps. Palm oil is also a good choice for making laundry soap and even for soap for washing dishes. Because it is naturally solid at room temperature, palm oil is also excellent for greasing and flouring baking pans in the kitchen.

  Sustainable palm oil is available, but you have to make sure it is labeled as such.

- **Sunflower oil** — Sunflower oil is similar to olive oil, but it costs quite a bit less. It is a good moisturizer for your skin and also works well as a massage oil. This is also my primary cooking oil.

Waxes

Waxes are another popular ingredient in skin care products. Unlike oils, which tend to go rancid within a few months to a year at room temperature, waxes last a long time.

- **Beeswax** — In addition to being used to make candles and to polish furniture, beeswax is a popular ingredient in lotion, lip balm, soap, and other skin care products. It moisturizes skin by helping retain moisture and is also reputed to have antiseptic properties, historically being used for healing wounds.

- **Jojoba** — Although you often see the term "jojoba oil," jojoba is a wax, rather than an oil or a butter. Being a wax, it has a very long shelf life. It's liquid at room temperature and is very slippery, so it is great as a massage oil and used in skin care products. It is not digestible, however, so should not be used in cooking.

- **Lanolin** — My children grew up putting pure lanolin on their lips during our dry Illinois winters. The consistency is similar to petroleum jelly, but it comes from wool rather than petroleum. When wool is sheared from sheep, it is coated with lanolin, which must be washed off. A substance that comes from sheep may not sound appealing, but use it once on cracked and bleeding lips in the middle of winter and you will be singing its praises forever. I first learned about lanolin twenty years ago when I was a lactation consultant. Its healing properties seem to be nothing short of miraculous for anyone with damaged skin, whether it is a breastfeeding mom with cracked nipples or a construction worker with cracked elbows. Lanolin added to recipes makes a soap that even the driest skin can tolerate, although it seems like a waste to let it wash down the drain.

Butters

While oils contain only the oil from a plant, a butter may contain other parts or components of a plant, which is why it is not liquid at room temperature. In some cases, you will find an oil and a butter have been produced from the same plant, such as olive oil and olive butter or avocado oil and avocado butter. Typically, butters are used in body butters and scrubs, while oils are used in soap recipes.

- **Cocoa butter** — I started adding this to my castile soap recipe because I wanted a harder bar that would not dry out my hands and this accomplished both of those goals. Cocoa butter is one of the few oils or butters that can be purchased non-deodorized, but don't get your hopes up about making your soap smell like chocolate. It is used so sparingly in most soap recipes that the fragrance of the cocoa is diluted and lost. Cocoa butter can be temperamental, separating when mixed with some oils, so it is not always a good choice for making creams.

Makeup Remover

Unrefined, unscented shea butter is very pure, natural and gentle — much nicer, in my opinion, for using on the face (especially the eyes!) than commercial cold creams or makeup removers. I simply take a small amount of shea butter, rub it onto my fingers, then gently massage onto my face. Use a warm wet cloth to remove all traces of both shea butter and makeup. It is essentially a more natural, but just as effective, version of an old fashioned cold cream.

— Maggie Howe, Adel, Iowa

 Shea butter — I first used shea butter in a sugar scrub and I was an instant fan. It melts on contact with skin and is an excellent moisturizer. It is best to use shea butter in recipes that do not require melting because that can cause it to become granular, which does not feel nice when rubbed into your skin. When buying shea butter, ask the supplier if they melt it during packaging, and avoid buying from suppliers that say yes. Most know that melting will cause graininess and will avoid the practice.

Creams and moisturizers

Creating a product that works for you is really a matter of figuring out which oils and butters have the properties that suit your skin. Typically, people with drier skin prefer butters, and people with normal skin or combination skin prefer lighter oils, such as grape seed or sunflower oil. If you have oily skin, you may not need to put anything on it to keep it from drying out. Even dry skin may improve dramatically if you simply try a soap that is gentler. Because we've all been exposed to advertising that leads us to believe we have to use complicated products to stay beautiful, the idea that skin may need no additional moisturizer or only needs a single oil seems too simple.

I typically start with something that I already have on hand and go from there. If you have sunflower oil in your pantry, try that. You won't have to buy anything special if you like the result. For something that's more moisturizing, try jojoba or olive or grape seed oil or one of the butters, such as shea butter or avocado butter. Cocoa butter is rock solid at room temperature so if you want to use it in a cream, you have to melt it and mix it with a softer butter.

There are commercial creams and lotions, and some companies market moisturizers, which can be either. The main difference between a cream and a lotion is that a lotion has a larger amount of water, which makes it easier to spread across your skin. It appears white because the oil and water have been emulsified by the addition of an emulsifying agent to prevent separation. I don't make any lotions because once you add water, you introduce a medium for bacteria growth, which means you have to add a preservative. Many times alcohol is also added, which has a drying effect on the skin. When making your own, however, you can use only the purest ingredients and avoid the need for chemical preservatives.

Body Butter

2 ounces shea butter

1 ounce avocado butter

1 ounce apricot kernel oil

1 ounce sweet almond oil

a few drops essential oil (optional)

Weigh all the ingredients on a digital scale and then mix together using either a mixer or a fork. Add essential oils for fragrance or aromatherapy benefits, and mix well.

Savings: This body butter is similar to a high-end cream that boasts 25 percent shea butter and retails at $42 for seven ounces. This recipe, which has 40 percent shea butter, costs $1.65 to make five ounces, not including the essential oil.

Soaps

People have been making soap for thousands of years. It was not until the 1800s that soap became big business. Prior to that, it was made from waste products that were available in any home — some type of fat plus lye that was made from ashes in the fireplace. Soap varied around the world depending on the type of fat available locally. Most homesteads in North America used lard from pigs or tallow from cattle; people in the Mediterranean used olive oil, and people in Indonesia used tropical oils, such as palm. As discussed in the oil section, there are drawbacks to using only one type of oil to make soap. Today we can combine oils based on what we know about their benefits, and we can have soaps that are mild and long lasting.

Most of the bars of "soap" in the store are not really soap. They are actually detergents, and in fact, advertising campaigns have even focused on the difference, claiming that soap leaves a film on your skin that the advertised product does not. The message in the advertisement is that a soap film on the skin is a bad thing, but nothing could be further from the truth. When soap is superfatted with oils, it leaves the extra oil on your skin, which keeps skin from drying out. Before I started making my own soap, I had a bottle of liquid soap next to the sink, as well as a bottle of lotion. I needed to use lotion after washing my hands through the day because the commercial soaps dried out my skin so badly. Provided it is made with excess oil, natural soap doesn't do that. After switching to naturally made soap, many people have found that they are able to eliminate their use of lotion. Homemade soap can be specifically formulated for hand washing, for bathing and showering and for washing your face, and, of course, problematic ingredients for those with allergies can be left out. In spite of having allergic reactions to many commercial soaps, I'm able to use a variety of essential oils in my soaps without any problems.

Although the idea of making your own soap may sound intimidating, it has been gaining in popularity in recent years. Recipes and instructions can be found online, as well as in books. It is becoming so popular, in fact, that I've seen some people blogging about it after making only

Savings: Savings will vary based on which soap you normally buy at the store, but going through twelve $4 bars of soap per year adds up to $48 a year. Making an equal amount of unscented homemade soap could cost as little as $12, depending on which oils you use, for a savings of $36 a year. As one of those people who had terribly dry skin when using commercial soaps, I also save an additional $15 to $20 a year because I no longer have to buy hand cream.

one or two batches of soap. As with everything else on the Internet, be sure the writer is knowledgeable about the subject.

Scrubs

Although soap does a great job of removing oil and dirt from your skin, it does not necessarily remove dead skin cells. To exfoliate your feet or your back, you can use a loofah, a natural sea sponge, a specially made buffing sponge, or a rough towel. A loofah can be grown in the garden, costing almost nothing and having no transportation costs. You can also use it for scrubbing pots and pans or your bathtub. It will even biodegrade in your compost pile when it is no longer useful.

There are natural substances that exfoliate just as well as expensive commercial products for the delicate skin on the face. My personal favorite is baking soda. That's the whole ingredient list. I keep a one-cup plastic container of baking soda in my shower. A couple of times a week after washing my face with my homemade soap, I scoop up a tablespoon or two of baking soda with my fingers, rub it between my hands until it's evenly spread out, and then I rub it across my face and neck. After three or four seconds of massaging all parts of my face and neck, I rinse off the baking soda in the shower. After my skin has dried, it is as soft and smooth as baby's skin.

A sugar scrub, which contains oils, is good for dry skin. Sugar scrubs are used on the back, hands, and other extremities, but I know some women who swear by using a sugar scrub on the face for very dry or mature skin. When you use a sugar scrub, you can generally forget about using anything for moisturizing afterwards because your skin will absorb the oil in the scrub. To use a sugar scrub, scoop up about a tablespoon of it

Shea Butter Sugar Scrub

3 ounces shea butter

2 ounces grape seed oil

2 ounces apricot kernel oil

a few drops of essential oil (if desired)

$\frac{2}{3}$ cup sugar

Weigh the butter and oils on a digital scale and mix together either by hand or with a mixer until well blended. Add the sugar and continue mixing until all the lumps are smoothed out.

Light Sugar Scrub

2 ounces castor oil

2 ounces apricot kernel oil

a few drops of essential oil (if desired)

1 cup sugar

Weigh the oils on a digital scale, pour them into a bowl, and stir to mix. Add the sugar and stir until blended.

Because castor oil is reputedly anti-fungal, this is a great scrub to use for your feet, especially when combined with tea tree oil or peppermint essential oil.

Salt Scrub

3 ounces sweet almond oil

2 ounces avocado oil

a few drops of essential oil (if desired)

1 cup natural sea salt (non-iodized)

Weigh the oils on a digital scale, pour them into a bowl, and stir to mix. Add the salt and stir until blended.

and rub it on the skin that you want to treat. Rinse with either plain water or soap, depending on how much of the oil you want left on your skin.

Some people prefer salt scrubs to sugar scrubs, but this is largely a matter of personal preference. Salt is reputed to draw out toxins and impurities. Keep in mind, however, that if you have any broken skin, salt will sting.

Keep a small amount of a homemade scrub in a jar on the bathroom counter for regular use, and store the rest of it in the refrigerator because most of these oils go rancid within a few months if left at room temperature.

When you begin making your own personal care products, either buy new containers from soap supply companies or repurpose containers that held similar products. Be sure to thoroughly wash containers before reusing, even if they held your naturally made scrubs or butters, because leftover oil will turn rancid and ruin the new mixture.

> **Savings:** Commercial scrubs can cost anywhere from $7 to $70 for a jar or tube, compared with the Salt Scrub recipe that will cost about $2 or the Light Sugar Scrub, which will cost $1 per batch. Using baking soda as a scrub will cost you less than a penny per use.

Toners

Has anyone else noticed how toners have disappeared from many cosmetic lines? I remember a cosmetic salesperson telling me that if I didn't use a toner after washing my face, it would be like not rinsing my dishes after washing them. Many experts, today, however, say that a toner is unnecessary at best and may actually cause problems by drying out your skin. But there are natural options available for those who need a toner. Witch hazel can help to remove oil from skin when it feels like soap is not doing an adequate job of cleaning. If you have trouble with acne, many people swear by 3 percent hydrogen peroxide, which is inexpensive, available in most grocery and drug stores, and is similar to benzoyl peroxide. A lot of acne is caused by bacteria, which peroxide kills. However, it will kill all bacteria on your skin, and that is not necessarily a good thing, so it should only be used when needed for treating acne. Repeated use of hydrogen peroxide can bleach hair and eyebrows, so be careful when using it. If you feel the need to close your pores after washing, which some toners claim to do, simply splashing or misting cold water on your face will serve the same purpose.

> **Savings:** You can save as much as $200 a year depending on which commercial toner you used. Using tap water in a spray bottle for misting your face will save $11 for every five-ounce can of one popular brand that you don't buy.

Shampoo

It can be exhausting to attempt to find a shampoo that does not have lots of multisyllabic ingredients. Even though the industry insists that these ingredients are safe, if people are debating the safety of the chemical ingredients, I'll go with natural ingredients that I know are safe. When I mentioned this topic on my blog and Facebook page, I was surprised at how many people responded with other ideas for cleaning hair naturally.

I've used my homemade body soap to wash my hair with great results, but some people prefer using a bar of soap specifically formulated to create lather when rubbed all over the head. Most recipes for shampoo bars contain about twice as much castor oil as soap recipes, and they also tend to go lighter on the coconut or palm oil while including some of the more exotic and nourishing ingredients, such as jojoba, beeswax, shea butter and cocoa butter.

Very oily hair might need a second wash or a tablespoon of baking soda rubbed into the scalp to clean oily hair effectively. Try using only a body or shampoo bar first, however, because baking soda really sucks out the oil. I was shocked to see that I had frizzy hair after using baking soda and soap together, so I don't do that anymore. But if you have oily hair like my daughter, it might work very well for you.

Plain baking soda can be used to wash your hair. I was surprised at how silky and soft my hair felt after using only baking soda. Some people don't use anything at all to wash their hair. They simply run water through their hair while in the shower, and they report that their hair looks and feels fine. This works best for people with dry hair and especially for post-menopausal women who tend to have drier hair.

If your hair looks good and feels good after washing with a natural product, you may not need a conditioner. However, if you are unhappy with the appearance, or you have trouble styling your hair, you can try a couple ounces of vinegar diluted in water as a rinse. Some people swear by apple cider vinegar, but any type of vinegar will work. And no, you will not smell like a pickle forever. The smell of vinegar dissipates quickly.

> **Savings:** Most shampoo bars cost about $1 each to make and will last about as long as half a bottle of shampoo. Depending on whether you buy your shampoo at the discount store or a salon, you could save anywhere from $1 to $20 on a bottle of shampoo, and you won't be sending all of those plastic bottles to landfills or recycling facilities.

Dental hygiene

I remember being told as a child that if I didn't brush my teeth daily with toothpaste, my teeth would rot and have to be pulled by the dentist. And as proof, my mother pointed out my grandmother, who had no teeth. So every day, without giving it much thought, I brushed my teeth. It never occurred to me until recently that I should look at the ingredients in my toothpaste as carefully as I look at the ingredients in my food. Although we don't technically ingest toothpaste, some of it can be absorbed into our bodies through the mucosa of our mouths.

As it turns out, there are a number of potentially harmful ingredients in toothpaste and even more ingredients that have never been tested for safety. While many of us have been avoiding sodium lauryl sulfate in our shampoo for years, we had no idea it was also in many popular brands of toothpaste. PEG-6, polysorbate-80, and benzoic acid are a few other common ingredients that are known to be toxic.[7] Polyethylene glycol is an ingredient commonly found in both toothpaste and antifreeze.

Although there are commercial toothpastes available that don't have these ingredients, they can be pricey, and there are natural and inexpensive alternatives. Some people swear by baking soda. Adding a bit of xylitol, which is a natural sweetener that does not cause cavities, will reduce the salty taste. Xylitol can be purchased online and in health food stores.

Dr. Gregg Schneider, a dentist in Rahway, New Jersey, says that baking soda mixed with hydrogen peroxide makes a good toothpaste. "Baking soda is mildly abrasive so it is effective in plaque removal. It neutralizes bacterial acids that damage the enamel, and it is antimicrobial. You would not want to use a strong abrasive on the teeth because you would wear away the enamel. Hydrogen peroxide aids in removing the plaque from the teeth."

Dr. Sanda Moldovan, a Los Angeles periodontist specializing in integrative oral health medicine, says that we really don't need to use anything at all when brushing our teeth because it is the action of the bristles on the toothbrush that actually cleans the teeth.

Savings: A tube of toothpaste with all natural ingredients costs $4 to $5, and depending on how much you use and how often you brush, a tube will last a month or two, adding up to $24 to $60 a year. Brushing your teeth with baking soda from the big box that you've already purchased for other tasks, will cost you less than a penny a day.

Deodorant and antiperspirant

In spite of claims that underarm antiperspirant is harmful to health, it is still used because we think we need it. Of course, no one wants to stink, but there are natural alternatives that work for most people. I had periodically used plain alcohol under my arms over the last twenty years, but I didn't do it regularly because I was worried about it drying out my skin. I also felt guilty about tossing a cotton ball in the garbage with every application.

Two years ago I decided that I shouldn't make a decision based on assumptions, and I started using alcohol daily to see what would happen. To eliminate the waste factor, I put the alcohol in a spray bottle and put a squirt under my arms every morning. It worked perfectly well as a deodorant where it hit the skin, but I wasn't getting full coverage with a single squirt, so I cut the alcohol by 50 percent and started using two squirts. If I feel like I missed a spot, I will do a third squirt. After a couple of months I also added a few drops of lavender essential oil simply because I like the way it smells.

I also realized that I didn't need to use my deodorant spray on days when I'd showered first thing in the morning. Bacteria cause underarm odor, so if you do a good job of washing under your arms, there won't be any bacteria there until you have been sweating for a few hours. The other thing I've learned is that if you sweat a lot — as in sweat pouring off your body as you work outside in the middle of the summer — you don't stink. When the sweat is pouring off your body, it doesn't sit under your arms, where the bacteria can grow. Your clothes, however, are a different story. Once they're soaked in sweat, bacteria starts to grow, and by the next morning your clothes can be quite smelly. Since most of us are able to shower on a regular basis and have clean clothes to wear daily, deodorant is not as necessary as advertisers would like us to believe.

If you don't like the idea of using alcohol, try using baking soda or apple cider vinegar. Alcohol works because it kills bacteria, but you can also create an unfriendly environment for bacteria by using baking soda or vinegar, which each work by pushing the pH either too high or too low for the bacteria to thrive. There are also a multitude of deodorant recipes online that make a paste out of baking soda and coconut oil or one of the other oils discussed earlier. People who use these say that a tiny amount is all that is needed to avoid odor. I have tried using a variety of other oils under my arms and discovered that they also eliminate odor, even without the baking soda.

What about antiperspirants? Trying to stop your body from performing a natural function falls into the category of messing with Mother Nature and usually doesn't have a positive result. Although research results have been mixed on whether antiperspirants cause breast cancer, it seems prudent to avoid using something that really isn't needed. Regardless of whether they use an antiperspirant, most people who work in an office don't sweat much. And people who work outside have sweat pouring off the entire body, so there does not seem to be much point in stopping one small area from sweating.

Dress shields, also known as clothes shields, can be used to deal with a serious problem of sweating under the arms. There are disposable and washable varieties available, but of course, disposable products are not ecothrifty. The washable varieties either pin to the clothing or strap onto your arm and shoulder with an elastic band. You can also buy undershirts or camisoles with the shields already sewn into place, and you can find them with various levels of absorbency.

> **Savings:** Commercial deodorant costs $3 to $9 per container, and an equal amount of baking soda, alcohol, or oil will cost you less than $1. The alternatives to deodorants and antiperspirants are so inexpensive that by switching to a natural one, you almost completely eliminate the cost from your budget.

Shaving

The obvious ecothrifty choice for shaving is to stop doing it. But it's not possible for some men, such as firefighters and those in the military. And it may not be the most comfortable choice in the middle of a hot summer. In my quest to find an ecothrifty shaving alternative for my husband, I began looking for a non-disposable razor online. First I searched for straight razors, which can be sharpened and honed and with good care will outlive the owner. Aficionados of straight razors swear a good one will provide a closer shave than any disposable razor on the market because they can be angled to glide smoothly across the face. Because of the safety shield, a disposable razor can be held against the skin at only one angle.

Although a straight razor is definitely an earth-friendly choice because it will not contribute to the two billion disposable razors that go to the landfill every year, it didn't seem to be a frugal choice. The best ones cost a few hundred dollars. When I asked men about the quality of the less expensive ones, they said they did not last and didn't provide a close shave. When you actually do the math, however, the straight razor does pay for itself over time.

Coming in at second place for an ecothrifty shaving option is a non-disposable safety razor. I had no idea these were still around, but like the straight razors, they have an enthusiastic following, and they are not difficult to find online. The razor handle and the part that holds the blade are made of metal and will last for years. Only the double-sided metal blade is disposable, but it is very thin and can be purchased in packages of ten, reducing the amount of packaging that goes into a landfill. The razors generally cost $30 to $100, depending on brand, and the replacement blades can be purchased online for 50 to 75 cents each.

The propellant-filled cans of shaving cream are neither earth friendly nor wallet friendly, but you have to put something on your face if you

A double-edge safety razor is a single blade razor that enthusiasts insist gives a closer shave than its double- and triple-bladed, disposable counterparts.

Shaving sets with a double-edge safety razor, shaving soap, and a brush make a nice gift. When buying a shaving brush, be sure to buy one that comes with a stand, which allows it to dry with the bristles pointing down to maintain its shape.

are using a straight razor or a safety razor. Logically, this process is called wet shaving. For a couple of centuries, men used a shaving brush and a bar of soap to lather up their faces before shaving. Using a brush to create suds on your face makes the hair soften and stand up, ready to be sliced off by the razor. Although you can spend as much as $20 on a tub of traditional shaving cream, a bar of soft soap will work, and if you make your own soap, you can find recipes for shaving soaps online.

Electric shavers may be an ecothrifty alternative to disposable razors if they are corded and do not have a rechargeable battery. Although they use very little electricity, rechargeable shavers have a battery, and, unfortunately, there have not been any batteries invented yet that are environmentally friendly. When the battery can no longer be recharged, it has to be replaced at a qualified service center. Also, the quality of electrical appliances in general has been going down in recent years. One reason my husband quit buying electric shavers is because they didn't last more than a couple years before going to the landfill. Although one of the more expensive models may last longer, they are definitely not frugal with a price tag of a couple hundred dollars, and they may or may not last long enough to pay for themselves. Some also come with disposable cleaning cartridges that will cost around $60 a year.

> **Savings:** I had no idea this would be so challenging to calculate, but when I asked men how often they replaced their disposable razors, the answers ranged from every few days to every few months! And to complicate matters even more, the cost of disposable razors varies from 50 cents to $4 each. Because the majority of men said they used a new razor every week or two, it seems that most could save about $50 a year on disposable razors by switching to one of the non-electric alternatives.

Feminine products

Sanitary pads, tampons, and personal lubricants, like many commercial products, did not exist a century ago. By 2015, feminine hygiene product sales globally are expected to gross $14.3 billion annually.[8] One reason it is such a lucrative business is the products are almost exclusively disposable or consumable, which makes it essentially recession-proof. Women think they have no choice other than to buy the products month after month. But there are alternatives.

Menstrual supplies

An often overlooked way to save money is to stop buying sanitary pads and tampons month after month. Fabric pads, natural sponges, and menstrual cups are growing in popularity for many reasons. Over the course of a woman's life, she will have more than four hundred monthly periods and could send thousands of used pads or tampons plus packaging to landfills and into sewer systems. And consider all of the resources put into manufacturing those products and the fuel required to deliver them to warehouses and stores. There are alternatives that will save money and reduce garbage.

Reusable pads are available commercially, and although it may seem they are expensive initially at $12 to $15 per pad, they will pay for themselves in a year or two, and they will last for ten years or more. If you choose to make your own, using patterns available online, they'll pay for themselves even more quickly. Users of commercially available pads made of cotton flannel say that the pads are more comfortable than the disposable ones made of plastic and paper and that skin rashes do not occur with cotton pads. Many women also report shorter, less painful periods after switching from disposable products.

With so many positive attributes, why don't more women use reusable pads? Probably the main reason is the "ick" factor, although some may also view it as an inconvenience and would rather toss a blood-soaked pad in the garbage. Most women, however, do not toss blood-stained panties in the garbage. Caring for reusable pads is no different than caring for blood-stained clothing. While some women soak the pad in a bucket as soon as it is removed, others simply wait until doing laundry and then prewash the pads in cold water before laundering with towels or clothes. If you soak the stained pads in a bucket, you can pour the bloody water down the toilet, or you can use it to water houseplants, giving them a nutritional boost naturally.

Menstrual cups and natural sea sponges offer internal solutions for dealing with your period. This can be a less expensive option than commercially made pads. A cup or sponge can be washed and reused immediately, so you only need one. The cup is probably a better option for women who must use public restrooms because it can be emptied and reinserted without washing. If you prefer the sponges, buy two or three to keep in a plastic bag in your purse so you can insert a clean sponge and put the used one in your purse.

When you buy reusable feminine products, you never have to worry about running out of sanitary products. If you use a cup, you don't have

---

The decision to use reusable pads was an easy one. Disposable pads were incredibly uncomfortable. I was never able to find a brand that I liked and spent too much money trying to find one. I found someone on Etsy who made reusable pads and placed an order. Not only are the pads comfortable, but they are really cute, too! Who would have thought that pads could be cute!

— Heidi Nawrocki, Lumberport, West Virginia

to remember to put disposable products in your purse after your period starts. And because the cup won't dry out the vagina like tampons do, it can be inserted when you are expecting your period to start.

> **Savings:** You can save $50 to $80 a year, depending on how heavy your periods are, if you stop buying disposable feminine hygiene products.

Personal lubricants

Commercially available personal lubricants are generally made with a complicated list of chemicals, including propylene glycol, which is a known allergen that causes contact dermatitis in some people. It is also used as an automotive antifreeze and de-icer. We are probably not talking about saving hundreds of dollars here by switching to a natural alternative, but some women have problems with recurrent yeast and bladder infections when using commercial lubricants, so if you fall into that category, you will save a lot more than dollars by switching to a natural alternative.

There is really nothing complicated about finding an alternative. Most plant-derived oils are slippery and work well as a lubricant. However, avoid using castor oil because it is rather sticky. Sunflower, olive, and grape seed oils work especially well. Because they are all natural, they are less likely to cause negative reactions. If you can consume a certain type of oil without a reaction, you can probably use it as a personal lubricant without any problems. So, if you're allergic to coconuts or peanuts, don't use those oils.

> **Savings:** Savings on this will vary from person to person based on usage, but you could save hundreds of dollars if that product has been causing health problems.

CHAPTER 2

Health and Fitness

Being ecothrifty does not just mean saving money while taking care of the earth. It also means taking care of yourself in a sustainable manner. Ignoring your diet, activity level, and health is not sustainable. In this section, we'll talk about how to take care of yourself and keep yourself healthy without using a lot of commercial products.

Drugs

There are 1.2 billion visits to doctors' offices, outpatient clinics, and emergency rooms per year in the United States, which amounts to almost four visits per person annually,[9] and one or more medications are prescribed in seven out of ten outpatient visits.[10] Many of those visits and prescriptions are unnecessary and possibly harmful. It is widely known that antibiotics do nothing to fight a viral infection, yet many patients want antibiotics to treat a sore throat or cough, and many doctors are willing to oblige. Upper respiratory infection is the number one reason children are prescribed medication,[11] although viruses cause many of these infections.

What's wrong with taking drugs that you might not need? Obviously, it is a waste of money. But it's also bad for you and society because it leads to more antibiotic-resistant strains of bacteria.

Educating yourself about your medical condition is key. Rather than assuming that you need medication, do some research and ask your doctor if a medication really will help your condition. Some doctors offer a prescription because they assume the patient expects it.

Alternatives

When we don't feel well, we want to improve the situation as soon as possible, which is understandable. However, that does not always mean that a trip to the doctor or a prescription is the answer. There are natural alternatives available that are inexpensive and sometimes practically free.

Colds

Americans spend $40 billion a year on medications to alleviate the symptoms of the common cold, even though research does not show that it is beneficial. Most people will improve within a week to ten days, regardless of whether they take over-the-counter or prescription medication.[12] In fact, some of these drugs, such as antihistamines and cough suppressants, may be doing more harm than good in the long run. Antihistamines dry up your nasal passages, making it harder for your body to expel the mucous that is making you feel so miserable. Cough suppressants are working against your body in a similar way, keeping your body from coughing up mucous.

There are free natural alternatives that can help you feel better.

- Take a hot shower or bath to help with sore muscles and a congested head. I am always amazed at how much better I feel after a hot bath.
- Put a couple of inches of water in a pot and heat until it is steamy; then inhale the steam. This helps to clear your sinuses. It works especially well if you place the pot of steamy water on a table and put your head over the pot with a towel covering your head to trap the steam. If it feels too hot, lift the edge of the towel to let some heat escape.
- Drink warm liquids, such as herbal teas and chicken soup. This helps you breathe easier by thinning mucous.

- Avoid dairy products, which tend to create more mucous.
- Rest helps keep your immune system strong and helps it fight the infection.

> **Savings**: A box of 20 decongestant tablets costs about $10 online, whereas a box of 20 herbal tea bags is $2 to $3.

Constipation

The number one digestive problem in the United States, chronic constipation, affects 15 to 20 percent of the population and results in 2.5 million doctor visits.[13] Annually, $22 million is spent on prescription medications and another $660 million is spent on over-the-counter laxatives.[14] Unfortunately, medication is only a temporary solution for this problem.

The majority of constipation cases could be cured by an improved diet with whole grains, raw fruits, and vegetables eaten daily. Most Americans have a diet that is far too low in fiber-rich fruits, vegetables, and grains. Based on purchasing data, Americans consume about ten servings of grains per day, but only one serving is whole grains, which contain fiber. In a food survey, 40 percent said they did not consume any whole grains in a day.[15] Raw fruits and vegetables are especially important because cooking destroys fiber. In addition to reduced constipation, diets high in fruits, vegetables, and whole grains are also associated with reduced risk of heart disease, cancer, obesity, diabetes, and other diseases.

> **Savings:** A commercial laxative can cost anywhere from $4 to $26 per bottle, depending on the brand. By replacing low-fiber foods with fiber-rich foods, you can completely eliminate the cost of laxatives.

Herbal supplements

Whether you use herbs exclusively or as a complement to conventional medicine, you know that those little capsules can be expensive. However, there is an alternative. You can buy herbs in bulk and put them into gelatin capsules yourself. If you are already taking herbs, check the label to see how much of the herb is in each capsule. Most herbal capsules weigh around a quarter to half a gram. That means that a bottle of one hundred capsules contains about two to four ounces of a herb. For about the same price as a bottle of herb capsules, you can buy a pound of loose herbs and a supply of capsules to fill yourself. Although there are devices on the market that supposedly make it easier to fill capsules, they are not necessary.

Herbal supplements can also be taken in the form of a tea. Making a herbal tea with herbs bought in bulk saves the purchase of gelatin capsules. And buying herbs in bulk has the added advantage of reducing the number of plastic bottles headed to landfill sites.

> **Savings:** Although the savings will vary depending on the particular herb, you can save 75 to 90 percent by buying loose herbs and filling your own capsules. For example, a bottle of thirty 250 mg turmeric capsules costs $20. A pound of turmeric is $10.50. There are only 2.64 ounces of turmeric in the capsules, which is the equivalent of $121.21 per pound of turmeric. Gelatin capsules cost a penny or two each, depending on the quantity you buy. You would save about $110 by purchasing the turmeric and filling your own capsules.

Exercise

Our lifestyle has become so convenient that it is bad for our health. The majority of us do not need to do anything physical on a daily basis other than walk from a car to a building, which means we have to contrive ways to get the physical exercise that our bodies need.

Prior to completely changing my lifestyle so that my daily life included a lot of natural exercise, I tried every modern exercise regimen known to city dwellers. I joined the Y, but didn't keep it up, so I thought I should buy a treadmill for the basement. I didn't continue using it but thought maybe a bike would be more to my liking. That didn't work either, so I decided to get an elliptical trainer. Are you seeing a pattern here? If you guessed that I didn't keep exercising on that contraption, you would be correct. I decided machines in the basement were boring, so I started walking around the neighborhood. After a few months, I couldn't force myself out the door any longer, but I was certain that a real health club membership was the answer! Guess what? I didn't keep that up either. And I was not alone. Most people don't continue with an exercise routine.

The problem with exercise routines is that they are contrived. We don't have to hop on a machine and spend half an hour biking or walking to nowhere, so it is easy to come up with excuses not to do it one day or the next day or the next. We have people to see and places to go, and we don't have time to waste exercising. One answer is to make exercise a part of your daily life. Use the stairs rather than the elevator. Make a commitment to walk or bike to wherever you need to go whenever possible. You can use a backpack for carrying items. Understand that it is okay if you need to bike to the store three times a week to buy groceries, rather than driving once and bringing home everything in the car.

If you have the self-discipline to work out on your own, there are plenty of ways to get more exercise, such as walking around the neighborhood, doing yoga with online videos, and weight lifting with items around the house, such as bags of pet food or cat litter. You can also pick up weights inexpensively at yard sales or find them free on Freecycle (page 173).

One of the simplest, most effective things you can do to lose weight is to start measuring and writing down everything you eat. A few potato

> **Savings:** You can save $300 to $800 a year by not joining a health club, plus you are saving the money for gasoline to drive there and the cost of the fancy exercise clothing you might feel the need to buy.

chips once a week is not going to sabotage anyone's weight, but if you sit down with a ten-ounce bag and eat half of it, that is a problem. If you put a handful of chips into a bowl and then put the bag away, you will be less likely to overeat. If you need the moral support that you might receive at a health club, you can join an online support group — you can find free ones on Yahoo! or Google Groups — or ask a friend to make you accountable by emailing you daily to ask for updates on what you are eating and how much activity you are engaging in.

The fact that this type of weight loss (or weight maintenance) plan is free probably leads a lot of people to think that it isn't as effective as a high priced gym membership or joining a weight loss program. However, people do not lose weight and keep it off unless they change their lifestyle. As soon as they go back to their former unhealthy eating and exercise habits, the weight comes back.

If you have a weight problem, you probably need to look at what you are eating. ACE-certified personal trainer Kelly James-Enger, co-author of *Small Changes, Big Results: A 12-Week Action Plan To a Better Life*, has written hundreds of articles about diet and exercise, and she says she can sum up all of them in four words: "Eat less, exercise more!" But she adds, "That's usually not what we want to hear! I recommend people make small, doable changes (drinking more water, adding more fruits and vegetables to their diet, walking more) that they can maintain and make habits. I lost fifty pounds more than twenty years ago and have kept it off, not because I diet but because I've stayed active and eat pretty well 80 percent of the time. (I leave plenty of room for goodies like pizza and chocolate.)"

Savings: One of the most popular weight loss programs in the United States averages about $20 per week, which adds up to more than $1,000 per year.

Babies

It was not until I became pregnant with my first child that I began to think about what I ate or what personal products I used. Like a lot of pregnant moms, I started reading books on pregnancy. Most of the books talked about the importance of nutrition and exercise. Knowing what a big difference those books made in my life, I often wonder where I would be today if I had never become pregnant. I started reading labels and was shocked to discover that the blueberry muffin mix I had been buying contained no blueberries, but it did contain other ingredients that I could not pronounce. When I found a blueberry muffin recipe in a cookbook, I realized that the mix saved me only a couple of minutes and that if I made my muffins from scratch, I would know what was in them — and one of the ingredients would be blueberries.

The really significant result of all the reading during my first pregnancy was that I no longer believed something was a good idea simply because everyone else was doing it. I started to question why people did the things they did. Towards the end of my first pregnancy, I was getting very frustrated with my doctor's attitude that I was an accident waiting to happen, and I was even more frustrated by his belief that he was going to take care of me — and that I didn't need to worry about making any decisions about my pregnancy or my baby. Three months before my due date, I decided to switch to a midwife. It turned out to be an excellent decision for many reasons, and I went on to receive midwifery care for all three of my pregnancies. In fact, I became so excited about natural childbirth that I became a certified childbirth educator and a certified lactation consultant and went on to work with pregnant and breastfeeding moms for nine years. Having midwifery care during pregnancy was responsible for changing a lot of my habits and attitudes because midwives are very concerned about nutrition and other lifestyle choices that affect your health and the health of your unborn baby. Although I didn't realize it at the time, the natural lifestyle I chose for my children was also ecothrifty.

Breastfeeding

You don't have to think very hard to realize that breastfeeding is an ecothrifty choice. It can be almost free and puts nothing in the landfill, whereas the alternative is costly and creates a lot of trash. There are hundreds of studies showing that breastfed babies are healthier than their formula-fed counterparts. The comparison is similar to that of natural foods and processed foods. When we start creating food in a lab, whether it's a box of cereal or milk for a baby, all of the same questions about nutrition and safety arise. Just as science does not fully understand why a carrot is good for the body, it does not fully understand why human milk is good for babies.

When scientists start breaking down foods and analyzing them trying to create nutritious food, there will be mistakes. For example, vitamins A, C, E, and selenium can either prevent or cause cancer in various parts of the body, depending on the dosage and how it is administered.[16] Because we lack knowledge about how various nutrients interact with each other and within the human body, experts recommend eating lots of fruits and vegetables, rather than taking a certain dosage of various vitamin pills every day.[17] Although there are plenty of studies that link a highly processed diet with a variety of medical problems and a more natural diet with improved health, more research is needed to figure out exactly which nutrients play what roles in preventing or causing diseases.

This makes it challenging to figure out how to create any processed food, and a replacement for human milk for babies is no exception. Indeed, every few years formula manufacturers are extolling the virtues of the latest addition to their product saying that it replicates human milk even more closely.

In the mid 1990s when I was working as a certified lactation consultant I would have strongly urged parents to use a commercially prepared formula if the mother was not going to breastfeed. At that time, it seemed like a better choice than using pure cow or goat milk because the formula companies were at least attempting to add or remove various components and nutrients to make the formula more like human milk. Today, however, the basic component of most formulas — cow milk or soy — is not the same as it was fifteen or twenty years ago. The cows are eating genetically modified (GM) grains and being injected with growth hormones, and the soybeans are genetically modified. No one knows the long-term effects of humans consuming GM foods, and there is a theory that growth hormones in milk may be contributing to the childhood obesity epidemic. Another problem with GM foods is that they contain DNA from other foods, which could cause an allergic reaction. For example, some soybeans have been genetically modified with Brazil nuts, and some people will have an allergic reaction to the soybean because they are allergic to the nut, not the soybean.[18]

Although organic baby formulas are on the market now, they are more expensive than non-organic, meaning they are not an option for everyone. And even if you buy organic, buying powdered rather than liquid formula may be advisable as the cans may be lined with Bisphenol A, or BPA. Although BPA has been used for more than fifty years, research within the past decade has shown that it leaches into food and drinks and has linked it to cancer, heart disease, obesity, and diabetes because it is an endocrine disruptor, meaning that it messes with your hormones. In 2008, Canada banned the use of BPA in baby bottles.[19] Babies who consume reconstituted powdered formula will consume eight to twenty times less BPA than those who consume liquid formula from a metal can lined with BPA.[20]

Savings: Formula costs about $1,500 per year,[21] which means breast-feeding can easily save parents $1,000 or more, even when factoring in the cost of a good breast pump, nursing bras, and other supplies for breastfeeding. If you have more than one child, many of those breast-feeding supplies can be used when nursing a second or third child, saving even more.

Diapers

As hard as some people try to argue against them, cloth diapers are definitely the ecothrifty choice for babies. Disposable diapers will cost $1,500 to $2,000 by the time a child is using the toilet, and if you use disposables that are biodegradable and not bleached with chlorine, you can spend up to $2,500.[22] If you have more than one child, start multiplying. On the other hand, two or three dozen cloth diapers will last through many babies and continue to serve you for dusting furniture or cleaning up spills throughout the years. The cost of washing those diapers is minimal, especially if you use homemade laundry detergent and hang them to dry on a clothesline.

There are so many options available today that you don't have to worry about how to fold the diapers or accidentally sticking your baby with a pin. Velcro or snap closures make cloth diapers as simple to use as disposables. You can buy traditional white diapers and covers, or you can make your diaper covers part of your baby's wardrobe because there are so many different colors and patterns available.

Savings: You can get started with two dozen diapers and six covers for as little as $100. By following the ecothrifty suggestions for laundry in this book, a load can cost as little as 30 cents, only adding about $30 to the cost of using cloth diapers for a year, and saving about $2,000.

Wipes

The obvious ecothrifty choice is to not use disposable baby wipes. If you are already washing cloth diapers, it makes for little extra work to simply toss a washcloth into the diaper pail with the diapers. The added benefit of avoiding disposable wipes is that you are not exposing your baby to all of the chemicals in the wipes. I found that a wet cotton washcloth did a better job of removing poop from a baby's bottom than the thin, smooth disposable wipes did.

Savings: Disposable baby wipes cost 4 to 10 cents each, depending on the brand. If you use even five per day, that easily add up to several dollars per week, which translates to as much as $182 per year.

Powder and cream

Whether you buy a commercial powder or diaper rash cream, the active ingredient will probably be zinc oxide. Unfortunately, there will also probably be additional chemicals and fragrances to which you may not want your baby exposed. Fortunately, there are simple natural alternatives.

- Lanolin, shea butter, olive oil, or a combination of oils, butters and waxes can help moisturize and protect a baby's bottom.
- Cornstarch works as a natural powder.
- Pure zinc oxide can be added to cornstarch for a powder, or to an oil, a butter, or a wax for a cream to create a more protective barrier between the diaper and your baby's skin. Zinc oxide can be purchased online in its pure form. Be sure to get one that is intended for cosmetic use rather than for a nutritional supplement. The particles in the cosmetic use zinc oxide are too large to be absorbed into the skin. You want it to stay on the surface of the skin as a barrier between the skin and the wet diaper.
- Calamine lotion is not terribly different from the zinc oxide creams and powders because calamine is zinc oxide with .05 percent of iron oxide added, giving the lotion its pink tint.

Savings: A four-ounce tube of diaper rash cream costs about $5, whereas four ounces of shea butter cost about $1.60. Zinc oxide costs $7 per pound, an amount that will last longer than your baby is in diapers and can also be used to make sunscreen. Cornstarch costs about $1 per pound.

Food

It is interesting that we live in a society that has this thing we call baby food, which is really just food that has been pureed, processed, put into tiny jars, and marked up several hundred or even a thousand percent in price. The global baby food market was worth $25 billion in 2008 and is expected to be worth $37.6 billion by 2014 with 37 percent of that money spent in North America.[23] When you look at the ingredients of baby food, the cost is truly astronomical. A box of organic baby oatmeal costs 40 cents per ounce, or $6.40 per pound, but organic rolled oats cost about $1.50 per pound, which means you are paying more than four times as much for the baby food label and a little extra grinding. A jar of banana baby food costs 30 cents an ounce, but it is not hard to find bananas that cost only slightly more than that per pound, meaning that banana baby foods cost almost ten times as much as fresh bananas, which have more fiber and nutrition because they have not been processed. Baby food, especially that made for older babies, may also contain added water and fillers, meaning that it has less nutrition than an equal amount of the same food eaten fresh. Baby food is essentially a convenience food, but many parents are led to believe there is something special about it. Although I raised three children from infancy to adulthood, I never bought or made "baby food."

In the 1950s marketers convinced mothers that they should start giving babies solid foods at a very young age, usually by two weeks of age, but sometimes as young as only a few days old. Newly created baby cereals and baby foods were pureed to avoid a choking hazard. In fact, baby bottles were developed for pureed food so that babies could suck down their carrots or applesauce. Eventually medical science completely turned around the recommendation for starting solids so early, realizing that babies need only breast milk for the first six months of life. By six months of age, babies are physiologically ready for additional food, and they are much more adept at manipulating food that is in the mouth. Babies tend to grab everything and put it in their mouths whether you want them to do so or not.

Around the middle of the first year, when babies are starting to show an interest in solid foods and are able to sit up on their own, you can simply offer them a tiny bit of mashed food, such as part of a banana or sweet potato. The first few times you offer it, you are simply gauging the baby's interest and ability to actually move food around the mouth and swallow it. Introducing only one food per week is recommended so that if a food causes an allergic reaction, it can be identified. Don't give the baby too much that first time — a tablespoon is plenty — because too much could cause a digestive upset. You don't need a fancy baby food puree machine or even a blender or food processor. A fork can be used to mash up many cooked foods, including butternut or acorn squash, carrots, and white potato, as well as the banana and sweet potato already mentioned. Regular applesauce purchased or made for the rest of the family can also be fed to babies, as well as regular cooked oatmeal. However, because grains are more likely to cause an allergic reaction and are harder to digest, it is better to add them to the diet after you have already introduced a few fruits and vegetables.

For most of the baby's first year, milk provides the majority of the necessary nutrients, and as the baby gets older, solid foods will gradually replace most of the milk. By the time our babies were a year old, they were eating almost everything the rest of the family was eating, except for small, hard foods that could be a choking hazard, such as nuts and raw carrots.

It is easy to incorporate baby's diet into the family meals. When introducing banana, slice off about an inch of it, mash it with a fork, and offer it to your baby. You can eat the rest of the banana. When you want to introduce sweet potato to your baby, bake sweet potatoes for the family's dinner one night. Cut off a small piece of sweet potato and mash it with a fork for the baby when you're eating. Store the rest of the sweet potato in the refrigerator for three or four days in a covered dish. For the baby's next offering of sweet potato, just cut off a small piece again, mash it and offer it to your baby. You can do the same thing for white baked potatoes, cooked carrots, and winter squash. There is no need for you to mash up several bananas or potatoes or squash and put them in the freezer in individual servings. Simply feed fresh food to your baby just as you feed the rest of your family.

Baby food is not ecofriendly. Because babies can eat foods that have been cooked for the rest of the family, almost every container of baby food represents wasted energy and resources except those used when traveling, which would represent a tiny percentage of current production. Even when traveling it is possible to order foods that could be fed to your baby, such a baked potato or sweet potato that you mash with your fork before feeding just as you would if you were home. Most baby food today is packaged in non-recyclable containers, rather than the glass jars of yesteryear.

> **Savings:** If you feed your baby two 70-cent containers of baby food every day the first month after starting solids, it will add up to about $40 for the month. As the baby eats more, the cost will continue to go up every month. If the baby is eating seven containers of the baby foods for older babies, with an average cost of 85 cents per container, the monthly cost will be $178.50. This cost can be eliminated almost completely if you simply avoid buying baby food.

Walkers

A quarter century ago when I was pregnant with my first child, the experts said that parents should not buy a baby walker for their infants. Fast forward twenty-five years, and the research still says the same thing — children who use baby walkers actually will walk later than children who do not use them, and they actually will be at higher risk of injury. Babies in walkers are more likely to drown in a bathtub or swimming pool, get burned when grabbing a pot handle or pulling a tablecloth on top of themselves, or the most common, fall down stairs. Because a baby in a walker can move three feet per second, the vast majority of injuries happen when parents are watching. They simply cannot respond fast enough to prevent an injury. The American Academy of Pediatrics has even called for a ban on baby walkers.[24]

The ecothrifty choice is to not use a baby walker. It is safer and healthier for your baby, keeps one more plastic thing out of the land-fill, decreases the demand for more to be produced, and saves you the money you would be spending on the purchase. The same is true of the doorway jumpers, which also do nothing to help a child learn to walk.

> **Savings:** Not buying a baby walker saves $35 or more. And not buying a doorway jumper saves $20 or more.

CHAPTER 4

Clothing

A big part of being ecothrifty is not collecting more things than you really need. Planning is essential to the ecothrifty lifestyle. When you fail to plan your wardrobe, you tend to overbuy because you make poor choices. When I was a little girl, my parents would sometimes go out to eat at a buffet where there were far too many delicious looking choices, and I'd fill up my tray to almost overflowing and be unable to eat it all. And in my early adult life, I bought clothes the same way. I'd buy a blouse or a skirt or some other article of clothing simply because I loved the color or the design, giving no thought to what I had at home that might match it or even whether the color or design would look good on me. This practice meant I wound up with a closet full of clothes but often found myself saying, "I don't have anything to wear!"

How many clothes?

The first step in creating an ecothrifty wardrobe is to decide how many clothes you need. Working your way down the checklist, ask yourself what you honestly need. Feel free to cross out anything that you don't need due to geography or climate. For example, if you live in Hawaii, you probably don't need any turtlenecks. I could make suggestions for the number of each item needed, but I won't because this will vary from person to person. Although it might seem safe to say eight pairs of underwear (seven days in a week plus one extra), if you have a job or lifestyle that causes you to sweat a lot, you might wind up using more than one pair some days. It is your responsibility to be brutally honest with yourself about this. Don't try to justify four or five suits if you don't have a job that requires you to wear one every day.

I have not included things like swimsuits, outerwear, and raincoats because most people need only one unless you are a lifeguard or have a job that requires you to work outside daily. There are blanks at the end of the list where you can include clothing items that are specific to your job or lifestyle.

Make your list assuming you do laundry once a week. If you don't already do that, make a commitment to start. Most washing machines

Make sure you have clothing basics. This includes a blazer, a pair of jeans that are in good shape and in style, a white button-down shirt, a knee-length black skirt and a few other pieces. Sometimes it is hard for people to put things together in their closet because they are missing one or two key pieces that are foundation pieces for building outfits.

Pull out everything that still has a tag on it. About 90% of the closets I go into have clothes that still have tags on them. If you have made shopping mistakes in the past, get some of your money back by returning and/or consigning your clothing.

Realize that more clothes doesn't necessarily mean more choices. We think that having a closet stuffed full of clothes is going to make us happier, but in fact it may be limiting our choices. It's better to have four dresses you absolutely love than twenty that you are just "eh" about.

Only buy an item if it fits properly and if you absolutely love it. The idea is to make our closets personalized boutiques. Clothing will not change in your closet. If you buy a top that is a shade of green that is kind of off, it is still going to be kind of off four months from now. It won't change.

— Kaarin Moore, clothing consultant, Washington, DC

will hold about a week's worth of laundry, and if you let it build up over a longer time, it becomes intimidating and easier to procrastinate, which could ultimately lead to buying more clothes. Doing laundry only when the machine is full is an ecothrifty strategy that saves electricity.

There isn't a list for children because children outgrow their clothes so fast they don't really have the chance to wind up with a closet full of unused clothes. The point of this checklist is to keep you from over-buying.

Woman's Wardrobe

Need	Own	
___	___	T-shirts
___	___	Dress blouses
___	___	Turtlenecks
___	___	Sweatshirts
___	___	Sweaters
___	___	Blazers
___	___	Dress pants
___	___	Blue jeans
___	___	Casual pants
___	___	Shorts
___	___	Dresses
___	___	Suits
___	___	Socks
___	___	Underwear
___	___	Bras
___	___	Pantyhose
___	___	Gym shoes or sneakers
___	___	Dress shoes
___	___	Boots
___	___	Sandals
___	___	Belts
___	___	_____
___	___	_____

Man's Wardrobe

Need	Own	
___	___	T-shirts
___	___	Dress shirts
___	___	Turtlenecks
___	___	Sweatshirts
___	___	Sweaters
___	___	Sports coats
___	___	Suits
___	___	Ties
___	___	Dress pants
___	___	Blue jeans
___	___	Casual pants
___	___	Shorts
___	___	Socks
___	___	Underwear
___	___	Gym shoes or sneakers
___	___	Dress shoes
___	___	Boots
___	___	Belts
___	___	_____
___	___	_____
___	___	_____

After determining how many clothes you need, go through your closet and dresser and figure out how many clothes you own. Odds are good that you already have more than you need. But do you have the matching clothes, shoes, and accessories to actually wear everything? Set aside any lonely item that matches nothing. After finishing your inventory, ask yourself whether you should buy something to match the set aside piece so that you can wear it or whether you should take it to a consignment shop, donate it to charity, or give it to a friend.

Used versus new

When you do need additional clothes, should you buy new or used? When my children were young, I avoided thrift stores and garage sales until my frugal friend Sue mentioned that she often bought used clothing. Like many people I had the misconception that the only things to be had at such places were out-of-style bell-bottom jeans and mildew-scented suits. But Sue was always dressed up like a runway model, so I started to reconsider my aversion to second-hand clothes. Then she told me that when her son moved away from home and started buying new clothes, he discovered that he was allergic to the chemicals used on new clothing. He had to wash them multiple times before wearing them or else he would get a rash. He had never been exposed to these chemicals when he was growing up because his mother always bought used clothing.

When I told another friend that I was considering shopping at a garage sale, she said that she didn't like the idea of wearing clothes that had been worn by other people. However, many clothes in stores have been worn by others — sometimes tried on by several people — and not even washed before you try them on.

My attitude towards clothes has changed a lot in the last twenty years. I used to love shopping at the mall; today I find it about as much fun as a trip to the dentist. Buyers have to carefully check new clothes because the quality of garment construction varies. I've spent hours in stores reading labels for the past seven or eight years, and almost all of them are made in countries halfway around the world. If I can find one item in a store that was made in the United States or Canada, it is unusual. This can pose an ethical dilemma for the shopper who prefers to support domestic manufacturing or prefers not to support countries with less than ideal working conditions.

Shopping

Thrift stores are often run by charities that you may want to support, so shopping is a win-win situation for you and the store. When you shop at a garage sale or a locally-owned consignment shop, you know that the money is staying in your community rather than going to a multi-national corporation and supporting the economies of other countries. Consignment shops, which resell items for people, are more convenient than yard sales for both buyers and sellers. They have regular hours year-round like any other store, so buyers can shop when it is convenient for them, and sellers can drop off one item or twenty whenever they want to sell something. Although some consignment shops sell everything from clothing to housewares, others specialize, such as those that sell children's clothing.

We are social creatures and it can be fun to go shopping with friends, but it is a good idea to shop alone. When friends shop with you, odds are good that you will wind up buying something that you otherwise would not. Each of us has our own sense of style, and your friend's will be projected onto you. If you try on something that you are not completely in love with but your friend says looks great on you, would you put it back on the rack or buy it? Keep in mind that your friend will not be with you every morning in your closet when you are getting ready for your day. If you don't love it this minute, you won't love it tomorrow or next week.

Only go shopping when you have a goal and not simply because you received a coupon in the mail or noticed a big sale was on. If you need something specific, such as a white blouse or a dress, you can certainly take advantage of sales and coupons. But don't wait until the last minute because you could wind up buying something that you really don't love and will only wear once or twice. If you know you have an event coming up that will require a clothing purchase, start browsing in stores at least a couple weeks ahead of time so that you won't feel rushed or pressured into buying something less than perfect. Planning ahead also allows you to stop in at thrift stores two or three times to see if that perfect outfit has just been added to their inventory.

Swapping

Clothing swaps, sometimes called fashion swaps or clothes trades, seem to be gaining popularity. Basically, a group of friends gets together at someone's house, and each person brings clothes they want to trade. Some trades also include shoes, accessories, perfumes, and purses. Diane Tant's daughter Michelle Driver of Antioch, Tennessee, talked her into hosting a clothing swap at Diane's home in Franklin, Tennessee. "The best part was the fellowship. I think it was really enhanced by the wonderful food and drink — a real party atmosphere," Diane says. "I have people now begging me to have another one! And I will."

Michelle had been attending and hosting swaps about five years when she asked her mom to host one. "I would say about 90 percent of my friends who were invited were very skeptical. They thought that there wouldn't be anything that they would like or want since they themselves were bringing items that they were just, well, over. Since that first swap at my house, my friends have taken turns hosting swaps in their homes…. Each time, we've introduced the idea of a "fashion swap" to new friends and groups of people. I will definitely do it again — or have one of my friends do it. I think you need to have a good fashion swap at least once a year!"

Kaarin Moore, a clothing consultant, says planning ahead of time is critical for a successful event. Although you can have people show up and begin swapping right away, this strategy can create chaos. Kaarin suggests asking guests to drop off their contributions a couple hours ahead of the planned start time. Recruit some friends to help you organize things the day of the swap, and partner with a local business, such as a bar or restaurant, to offer a coupon for a drink or appetizer so that guests can mingle there before heading back to your place to begin picking out clothes.

"On a couple of occasions the swap has partnered with local shops by creating a guide of things to do in the neighborhood (and discounts for purchases with a special code) so people don't get bored between drop off time and swap time. The idea of partnering with local businesses expands the range of your swap and pushes some dollars to small business owners, which in turn builds a sense of community," Kaarin says. "It also opens doors to potential partnerships in the future."

Alternatively, food and drinks can be served outside in good weather, and guests can mingle there while you organize the clothes inside the house.

Tables holding clothes should be arranged so they are accessible from both sides. Portable clothing racks provide easy access to the clothes; just remember to ask guests to bring their clothes on hangers. Plan to use four or five rooms for displaying the clothes so people can look at them easily.

"We had all the clothing set up by category in a couple of rooms, and the jewelry, accessories, shoes, perfumes in another room," Michelle explains. "We had each person draw a number, and that determined which room number they would start shopping in. We gave about fifteen to twenty minutes to shop, try on, and decide which items they'd like to take from that room." Participants were limited to only three items during the first trip through each room. They could take five from each room on the second trip, and as much as they wanted on the third visit to a room.

Kaarin suggests that guests be given the rules ahead of time. "Are people allowed to bring winter clothes even though it is in the middle of July? Can you swap anything, or do people have to bring things that aren't damaged? Are participants allowed to take as many pieces as they want? Or, is it an equal trade for how many pieces they bring in — you bring in five, so you can take out five?"

Don't assume that no one will want a particular item just because you've fallen out of love with it. Michelle says, "I can't tell you how many times I've thought, 'no one will want this stuff! But I'll bring it anyway.' And I am always pleasantly surprised to see someone else bringing new life and enjoyment to a piece that had just worn out its welcome in my closet."

Finally, have a plan for disposing of the clothes that are left over. In most cases, people have decided that they don't want the clothes any longer, and the remains are donated to charity.

> **Savings:** In 2009, the average American spent $1,725 on clothing.[25] Excluding intimate apparel, socks, and hosiery, your clothing needs could be met by employing the ideas in this section, saving almost all of this annual expenditure amount.

Sewing

It might seem old fashioned, but like a lot of forgotten skills, some people are giving it a second look today. There are several benefits to making your own clothes, such as using exactly the fabric you want for the style of clothing that you love. You've probably said something like this when shopping: "Oh, I love this shirt, but I wish it wasn't this ugly color." Sewing your own clothes can be especially beneficial if your size falls between two commercial sizes.

Sewing patterns come in a variety of difficulty levels, so even if you have never sewn anything before, you will be able to find a simple pattern to start with. And if you don't want to learn to sew or don't have the time, ask around to see if you have any friends who sew. When a friend of mine was laid off from her job a couple years ago, she decided to do a few sewing projects, and I was a lucky beneficiary of her talent. She charged $20 an hour, and each thing she made took somewhere between two and four hours, depending on complexity. I paid in cash sometimes, and sometimes I bartered.

Second life for old clothes

It isn't terribly difficult to find ideas for turning old clothes into something new. People have been using tattered t-shirts and old diapers as rags for decades. If your blue jeans have holes in the knees, just cut off the lower two-thirds of the legs, and you'll have a pair of denim shorts. If they're torn higher up on the leg, you might be able to make a purse out of the upper portion of the jeans, and use strips from the legs to make a shoulder strap. A long strip of denim sewn into a tube and filled with uncooked rice, makes a heating pad that can be heated in the microwave. Smaller pieces of used denim or other fabric can be used in the same way to make hand warmers. In a later chapter, we'll talk about making quilts or rag rugs out of old clothes. You really are limited only by your imagination.

CHAPTER 5

Food

For more than a decade, organic has been at the forefront of what is considered healthy food. Although I would not argue that organic is better for the human body and the environment than conventionally grown food, it is not always the ecothrifty choice. The $5 frozen organic dinner is far from sustainable when you factor in all of the miles it has traveled from field to factory to store, as well as the layers of plastic and cardboard packaging. Recently, we have begun to realize that when it comes to food's environmental impact, local and unprocessed can be as important as organic.

The *Oxford American Dictionary* named "locavore" the word of the year in 2007, and since then, the local food movement has continued to grow. The number of farmers' markets increases every year, and farm-to-fork restaurants are starting to pop up in cities everywhere. At Station 220 in Bloomington, Illinois, the chefs are also the farmers, and at the Firefly Grill in Effingham, Illinois, you can see the garden where your salad was grown right outside the restaurant. Trolley Stop Market in Memphis, Tennessee, is owned and operated by farmers, who also operate a year-round farmers' market selling meat, dairy, produce, nuts, grains, and honey from farms in their area.

Determining the ecothrifty food choice can be complicated because it is not as simple as saying that the organic tomato costs more than the conventional tomato. The less expensive tomato may be the frugal choice, but it is not necessarily the ecofriendly or healthy choice. If either of the tomatoes is ripened on the vine, it will have more nutrients than a conventional tomato that is picked green and gassed with ethylene to turn red. The conventional tomato probably has pesticide residues on it. How many miles did either tomato travel to arrive at your supermarket or farmers' market? You may not always have the answers at your disposal when shopping at the grocery store. The hallmarks of ecothrifty eating are buying food that is locally grown, and organic when possible, and preparing most of your own meals. And it would be incorrect to assume that organic is always more expensive than conventional. Apples are just one example at my local grocery store. There is usually at least one variety of organic apple that costs the same or less than the conventionally grown apples.

Many people cite lack of time as the major deterrent to eating home prepared food. It is easy to get overwhelmed in modern society, and there is a business on practically every street corner ready to feed you twenty-four hours a day. But food choices have a great impact on the family budget and on the environment. You have three or more opportunities every day to make positive changes.

People think they can't afford to eat better. But we are spending less of our incomes on food today than ever before, and there are more overweight and obese people today than ever before. We are paying less for food, eating too much and unhealthily, and then spending money on health care and weight loss programs. Something is obviously wrong with this scenario.

Although we have made a great many positive advances over the past century, the changes made in diet have not been beneficial to eaters. But there is hope. You can improve your diet and save money doing it. Unlike making decisions about your house or your car, which you do every few years, you make decisions about your diet constantly. You can make changes gradually, incorporating a few new ideas every month. In fact, you are more likely to make permanent changes if you do it gradually, so don't feel like you have to change everything about your diet overnight.

Planning

Although it is easy to say that we are too busy to cook meals from scratch, the fact is that if we planned better, we would be able to cook more of our own food. Between slow cookers and bread machines, it is not difficult or time consuming to wake up to a hot breakfast or come home from work and have a hot meal waiting for you. But you have to plan. If you really don't like to plan, there are online services that will send you a menu and shopping list every week, but you can do the same thing for yourself, using menu items that you know your family enjoys. Start out by making a list of everything you like to eat for breakfast, and make another list for lunches and dinners. Include a list of nutritious snack foods, like nuts and fruit.

Next, make a menu for the week. Although you can do this on a plain piece of paper, I've found it more useful to put it in my planner so that I can see what needs to be done as I'm being reminded of everything else I have planned for that day. I was never very good at looking at a list on the refrigerator until an hour before dinner, which would be too late to fix something like pinto beans that should have been soaking all day. Online calendar programs will send you email or text reminders for food preparation tasks that need to be started earlier in the day.

Make a shopping list based on the menu for the week and shop for only those items. If you are not very good at sticking to a list when you do the shopping, ask someone else to do the shopping for you. I generally come home with lots of unplanned purchases, whereas my husband is completely blind to everything except what is on the list. The point here is that you should not put non-nutritious foods, like potato chips and candy, on your shopping list, and you should not buy them. Do follow the sage advice of never shopping when you're hungry. Patronizing a farmers' market rather than a grocery store will also help you to buy only nutritious foods because most of the items for sale there are real food.

Create a meal planning binder for organizing your weekly menus with corresponding shopping lists. This will save you time in the future because you can re-use them. There are online services that will email dinner meal plans at a cost of $60 or more per year, but you can create your own for free.

You might also consider buying small appliances to make it easier for you to cook more meals from scratch. A slow cooker, vacuum sealer, food processor, blender, or bread machine can help you achieve professional results in the kitchen. And they use a minimal amount of electricity — often less than a penny per use.

If you have a bread machine or a stand mixer with a dough hook, do not feel guilty about using it. I have heard people say they "cheat" by using one, but there is nothing wrong with saving time, especially if it means you are eating a healthier food with a smaller carbon footprint. In addition to being incredibly delicious, fresh bread is also better for the environment because you don't have the plastic bag that store-bought bread is packaged in, nor do you have the additional transportation involved in taking wheat to the bakery and then to the store. Naval submarines have long baked their own bread because it takes less space to store bread ingredients than it does to store bread.

Getting food

The most ecothrifty food is food you grow yourself. The second best choice is food grown by someone you know, whether it is a friend or a local farmer. Growing your own food or buying from local farmers or gardeners means you will be cooking from scratch as much as possible, rather than buying prepared food or convenience food. Not only is scratch cooking less expensive, but the meals will be more nutritious and contain fewer artificial ingredients. (Most of us don't have containers of diglycerides or xanthum gum in our pantries.) You will also be less likely to eat too much non-nutritious junk food. One reason we eat so much junk food in our society is because it is available everywhere. When I see a tasty dessert in the grocery store, I tell myself that I'll make it when I get home. Sometimes I do, but sometimes I forget about it, meaning that I've just saved myself a lot of empty calories, as well as the artificial ingredients that were in the prepared dessert and the money I would have spent on it. Homemade food costs a fraction of what prepared foods cost.

Eating seasonally is an ecothrifty strategy. Food that is local and in season has the smallest carbon footprint of any food option. It requires no canning, freezing, or dehydrating and no storage container. And when it comes to fruits and vegetables, if you eat them raw, you are getting all of the fiber and nutrients, making it the most nutritious choice. Grocery stores often have lower prices on produce when it is in season because it is abundant and needs to be priced to move through the store quickly. The same is true when you buy from local farmers because they don't always have facilities to store large quantities of produce.

But of course you can't always eat only foods that are in season. You can, however, preserve the harvest for eating during the rest of the year. Some people have told me that we have to import food into Illinois because we can't grow everything year-round. That would only be true if you wanted to eat raw foods year-round. In reality, most people are eating food that has been frozen, dehydrated, or canned commercially. It is more ecofriendly to preserve your own tomatoes in reusable jars than to buy canned tomatoes that traveled two thousand miles in cans that will either be recycled or sent to a landfill.

Avoid buying food that is sold in individual servings, such as yogurt, nuts, and drinks. You will save a lot of money and send less packaging to the landfill if you buy a quart of yogurt, for example, and dish out the amount you want. This strategy also saves money because you will wind up with less wasted food, especially if you have children who might not always finish a single-serving carton of yogurt.

Buying in bulk is another ecothrifty strategy that saves you money and uses less packaging. Although you might think that it would take you a very long time to use twenty-five or fifty pounds of a food, when we lived in the suburbs with three small children, we would use a twenty-five pound bag of brown rice every month. In our family of four adults today, we go through twenty-five pounds of flour every month. Baking four or five loaves of bread weekly and a few desserts monthly will use twenty-five pounds of flour. If you still think that you could not use a large quantity of a food in a timely manner, check with friends to see if they would like to split a bag with you.

Coupons

You might think that using coupons will save you money, but coupons are usually for processed foods, which will still cost more than a similar food made from scratch, even after deducting the amount of the coupon. Manufacturer's coupons are marketing tools used to introduce products to a consumer in the hope of creating a long-term customer. On the rare occasion that there is a coupon for something fresh, like strawberries, often it can only be used if you also buy a processed item, such as non-dairy whipped topping.

Purchasing a couple hundred pounds of meat at once means that you can almost never use the excuse that you have nothing to cook for dinner. Buying meat directly from a farmer not only saves money, but you will also know how the animal spent its life. You can ask the farmer about things that are important to you, such as antibiotic and hormone use, and ethical treatment of animals. Beef is usually sold by the whole animal, a half, or a quarter. Pork, which is a bit smaller, can usually be purchased as a whole or half animal. Lamb and goat, which are even smaller, can usually only be purchased as a whole animal. And don't worry — "whole" does not mean that you are butchering the animal yourself. More information on this is available in the "Freezing meat" section (page 64).

You may be able to buy heritage chickens or turkeys, as well as stew hens, which are laying hens that have passed their prime. Stew hens are usually far less expensive than other chicken because most people have no idea how to cook a stew hen, so the demand is low.

Keeping food

It can be really disheartening to buy a large quantity of food, only to see it go bad before you can use it, which completely negates any savings you might have realized. Some foods, such as beans, rice, wheat berries, and other whole grains will last forever in a pantry, but it is a good idea to keep them in a tightly closed container to avoid infestation by bugs, such as weevils. This is a good way to repurpose jars that originally held store-bought sauces and other food.

Canning

A great way to preserve the harvest from your garden or your local farmers' market is by canning food. Dismissed as old-fashioned not more than a couple decades past, today it is enjoying resurgence as consumers want more control of their food. BPA is found in hard plastic containers and the lining of cans used for commercially canned foods. Increasingly there are more plastic containers that claim to be free of BPA, but the metal can manufacturers continue to coat the inside of most cans with the substance.

A study published in 2011 that measured the amount of BPA in participants' urine after they ate canned soup for five days found the level increased more than a thousand percent.[26] The amount of soup they ate each day was only a single serving as defined on the can, and most participants complained that they were still hungry after eating it. Although the amount of BPA was back to pre-experiment levels five days after participants stopped eating the canned soup, what does this mean for people who eat canned foods daily? There is no definitive answer to this question, but if you don't eat commercially canned food, you don't have to worry about it. Keep in mind, however, that many restaurants use canned foods.

Cans are lined with BPA to resist corrosion, and even home canning has the potential to expose you to BPA because one-time-use canning lids are lined with BPA. The risk of contaminating food with BPA is not as great as with food in metal cans, however, because home-canned food rarely comes in contact with the lid. If you are concerned, though, reusable BPA-free canning lids are available. I began using them about a year ago, and they work quite well, although the canning process is different from one-time-use lids. Be sure to read the instructions on the box before using them.

Canning is environmentally friendly because you continue to reuse jars from year to year. If you also use reusable lids, you have zero waste.

You may be able to find used canning jars for sale in a classified ad or at a yard sale. If so, be sure to inspect them carefully for damage. If you can feel any imperfections when you run your fingernail over the glass, the jar should not be used for canning, but it can be used for storing grains, beans, and other dry foods.

Savings are greatest when you can vegetables or fruit from your own garden or orchard. And although the dollar savings are not as great when you buy fresh local produce to can, the benefits to the environment are the same and you will have complete control over the ingredients so you can avoid artificial ingredients and fillers.

There are two methods for canning. Foods that are high in acid, such as tomatoes, pickles, and fruits can be canned in a boiling water canner. The process is simple and usually takes fifteen to thirty minutes to process the jars. Low-acid foods, such as corn, beans, and meat, require canning at a higher temperature, which means you need to use a pressure canner, which is capable of heating the contents to 240°F. Boiling water canning is simpler and the equipment costs less to get started.

> **Savings:** The industrial canning process is a very efficient system, so the real savings with canning come from being able to preserve the foods that you grow yourself. You will be saving money if you have been buying some of the high-end organic pasta sauces that can cost as much as $6 to $8 a jar or salsas at $4 to $5 a jar!

Dehydrating

Although you can buy a fancy food dehydrator to dry your own food, there are a number of foods that can be dried in a more low-tech manner. Herbs, such as mint and basil, are probably the easiest to dry. Because they are thin and have low water content, they will dry at room temperature fairly quickly. I lay them in a single layer on a cookie sheet and put them inside an oven that is not turned on. To avoid mishaps, I put a sticky note over the oven control knob to remind everyone not to turn on the oven without removing the herbs. The note usually says something like, "Do NOT turn on!!!" The herbs are dried out and ready for storage when they crumble between your fingers. Store dried herbs in a jar with a lid. I usually don't crush them before storage, however, because the aroma and flavor will dissipate more quickly after crushing.

Smaller peppers can also be dried at room temperature, particularly cayenne peppers, which have very thin skin. The thicker the skin, the more problematic drying can be and the more important it is to hang them up rather than to attempt to dry them on a pan or countertop in a single layer. Jalapenos, for example, are more likely to mold than dry out if they are not hung with good air circulation on all sides.

Try this creative approach for tomatoes. Place thinly sliced tomatoes on parchment paper on a cookie sheet and dry them in a closed up car in the summer. In most parts of the United States in the middle of summer, the temperature in a parked car with closed windows can get up to 150°F to 170°F, which will dry out vegetables within a couple of days.

To dry peppers, tie a string around the stems and create a long rope of peppers. Hang it up out of the way where it won't collect too much dust.

Don't try this with herbs, though, because the temperature is far too high for drying them, and they will wind up brown and lacking in aroma within a day. You can store dried vegetables in a jar with a lid and use them in soups and quiches during the winter.

Savings: Sundried tomatoes can cost as much as $1 to $2 per ounce, but you can dry your own tomatoes practically for free.

Freezing grains

Minimally processed foods, like whole-wheat flour, should be stored in a freezer to preserve nutrients. Once wheat berries are ground, the oils are exposed to air and can become rancid. Storing them in a freezer slows down the aging process. It is also a great place to store grains and flour to protect them from being infested with weevils, beetles, or moths. If bugs have already infested your grains or flour, freezing is a non-toxic way to kill them. Flour should be stored in an airtight container in the freezer so that it doesn't pick up any odd odors or flavors.

Freezing meat

When you buy a meat animal or a part of a meat animal, the meat will need to be stored in the freezer. Unfortunately, some people don't like the idea of eating meat that has been frozen, which makes little sense in today's world. There is no difference in quality between fresh and frozen meat, although I understand that many people will argue that they don't like the taste of frozen meat. I think there are several reasons for this prejudice. First, the best cuts of meat are sold fresh, and people associate frozen meat with lower quality because cheaper cuts are sold frozen. The other thing that may contribute to the prejudice against frozen meat is that the quality of meat frozen in a home freezer can deteriorate.

Home freezers are not very cold, and they freeze the meat more slowly than the freezers at meat lockers. Quickly freezing meat preserves the quality. Also, if meat is not properly wrapped for storage, it will become freezer burned. I've never had a problem with freezer burn when meat has been wrapped and sealed commercially, and we've found some beef, chicken, and turkey in the freezer that was more than a year old. The type of wrap used by processors who freeze meat is different from the thin plastic and Styrofoam trays found in grocery store meat cases, which is only intended for short-term storage. Grocery store packaging does not protect the meat from air and will cause oxidation and freezer burn.

When you buy directly from the farmer, the animal is slaughtered around the time you purchase the animal or part of the animal. Most farmers don't send animals to the processor until they are already sold. The live animal is delivered with your name on it as the owner. This means that you decide how to have the meat cut and processed. If you like lots of ground meat, you can tell them you want fewer roasts, and they'll grind up those parts. You can tell them exactly how thick you want your steaks cut and whether you want your ground beef in one-pound or two-pound packages or some of each size. If you don't want sausage or bacon, they can make more steaks and ground pork from a pig.

Freezing produce

Freezing is probably the easiest way to preserve the harvest from your garden or the produce you pick up at the farmers' market when it is in season. Most fruits and vegetables freeze well. If properly stored in freezer bags or containers at or below 0°F, fruits and vegetables will last a year in the freezer. This means they need to be stored in a container without air. We resisted buying a vacuum sealer for longer than we should have. As a result, we had a lot of bags of green beans that wound up looking like blocks of green ice after only a few months. After we started using the vacuum sealer, however, green beans last for a year with no damage or decrease in quality. Don't worry about the cost of electricity when using a vacuum sealer. It uses about 100 watts total for the ten seconds or so that it takes to vacuum and seal both ends, so if you sealed five things per day, every day of the year, it would cost you 5 cents total for the year.

Most vegetables freeze well after blanching, which means being placed in boiling water for one to three minutes, followed by being plunged into cold water to stop the cooking action. The amount of time required for blanching varies from one vegetable to another.

Vegetables that freeze well after blanching:

asparagus	cauliflower	peas
broccoli	corn	potatoes (white)
Brussels sprouts	greens	tomatoes
cabbage	okra	turnips
carrots	parsnips	

Summer squash and green peppers turn to mush when thawed, so it's important to plan how you will use the thawed vegetable and prepare the frozen vegetable for that use. I shred zucchini for zucchini bread and freeze it in the correct quantity for the recipe, and I chop green pepper into strips and freeze them in small quantities to use in stir-fries and chili, although the crunchiness of a fresh pepper is definitely absent. When freezing tomatoes, I chop up a hot pepper and add it to a container of tomatoes that will be used for making chili.

There are a couple of options for freezing berries, and peaches can be frozen using these same techniques after peeling and slicing. To freeze berries and peach slices individually so they don't stick together, put them in a single layer on a cookie sheet in the freezer until frozen and then put them in a vacuum-sealed freezer bag or airtight container for storage. If you will be using them in cooking after thawing and don't mind the berries or slices sticking together, you can skip the step of freezing on a cookie sheet and put the fruit directly into the freezer bag, vacuum, seal, and then freeze.

Herbs can be frozen without blanching. Wash them, and when they are dry, store them in freezer containers or plastic freezer bags. Freezing will destroy the structure of the leaves, though, so they won't be crunchy or make a pretty garnish after thawing. However, they can be used to add flavor to foods that are being cooked.

> **Savings:** When strawberries are in season, they can be found for as little as $1 per pound in the produce section of my local grocery store. The regular price of frozen strawberries is close to $4 per pound.

Cooking food

Although lack of time to cook is one reason that almost half of our food dollars are spent away from home, there is another equally important reason — many people don't know how to cook. At least that's what food research tells us. And many of those who do cook view it as a weekend recreation similar to horseback riding, hunting, gardening, and other activities that everyone had to do historically but are no longer necessary in modern society. Apparently cooking from scratch has become so rare that researchers do not even bother following the trend any longer. They now define cooking as preparing food that involves some assembly of ingredients, which includes making a salad or a sandwich. In addition to so many meals being eaten outside the home, many of the meals eaten at home include frozen entrees and prepared foods. Food industry researchers are skeptical that cooking will ever again become a common event in the average household.[27] The situation is not that hopeless, though.

Cooking and finding the time to cook are only matters of learning new skills and organizing your time. With the right knowledge, you can be preparing more of your meals at home without spending any more time than you currently do driving to restaurants, waiting to be served, and waiting for your food. Fast food restaurants may be able to push something out the drive-through window in only a few minutes, but it is not exactly food. The products are filled with a multitude of multisyllabic ingredients — often two dozen or more in a single item, meaning you could consume close to a hundred ingredients in a single meal.

Keep in mind that it takes a bit of practice to master a new skill, and cooking is no different. Although it might take you a little longer the first few times you make something, you will be speeding through the process once you know how to do it. And not every meal has to be a

Mixes

You might be surprised to learn that I am not going to give you recipes for home-made mixes, such as biscuit mix or Cajun seasoning mix. In reality, store-bought mixes do not save you much time. While a recipe for a cake might have seven or eight ingredients, you will be adding three or four ingredients to a box of cake mix, which means it might save you one or two minutes. If you are making your own mixes, you still have to take the time to make the mix, so you really aren't saving any time at all, and you have to find a place and a container to store the homemade mix.

If you are tempted to buy store-bought mixes, restrain yourself. They tend to have many more ingredients than made-from-scratch alternatives, and many times they do not contain the ingredients that the label implies. For example, there is a commercial carrot cake mix that does not have any carrots in it.

---

big production. A grilled piece of meat and steamed vegetables take less than fifteen minutes to prepare.

I have always been a very busy person, regardless of whether I was working a full-time job away from home, running my own business, running a homestead, writing books, or some combination of the above, so I don't have hours a day to devote to preparing elaborate meals. Feeding my children frozen pizzas and fast food daily was not an option for me because I did not want them suffering from the same ill health I had as a child. That meant I had to figure out how to cook from scratch by finding every time-saving shortcut imaginable. This section provides instructions and basic recipes for saving time and money by making a variety of foods from scratch.

Breakfast

There are few things less nutritious than modern breakfast cereal, which is loaded with calories and artificial ingredients. When a group of researchers looked at the ingredients in eighty-four brands of breakfast cereals, they found that more than half of them contained more sugar than three chocolate chip cookies.[28] And it is overpriced when you look at the fact that the only real food ingredients are usually some type of grain and a sweetener. Luckily, breakfast is the easiest meal to improve when it comes to being ecothrifty and healthy.

Cereals

Grains provide hot and cold options for breakfast. Leftover brown rice makes a nice cold breakfast when you add a bit of milk with a sweetener and some fresh fruit. You can also make your own homemade granola, which you can eat with milk or yogurt. For a hot breakfast, oatmeal provides an endless array of options. One of my favorite combinations is chopped walnuts and maple syrup. Homemade jam also makes a nice addition to oatmeal, so you can have your own version of strawberries and cream or peaches and cream to rival the artificial quick oatmeal in the store. When I'm in the mood to be decadent, I add a tablespoon of peanut butter and about a dozen semisweet chocolate chips.

If you've never been a fan of the gooey rolled oats, you might try making oatmeal with steel cut oats. Steel cut oats have been cut (as the

Granola

Makes 10 cups.

½ cup butter (1 stick)	1 cup wheat germ
½ cup honey or maple syrup	1/2 cup wheat bran
½ cup water	1 cup seeds (pumpkin or sunflower)
6 cups rolled oats	1 tablespoon cinnamon (optional)
1 cup chopped walnuts or sliced almonds	

Melt the butter in a 5-quart Dutch oven over low heat, stirring regularly to keep the butter from scorching. When the butter is melted, add the honey and water, and mix well. Add all of the dry ingredients to the pot and stir until well blended. Divide the mix in half and spread each half evenly on a separate shallow baking pan. Bake in a 250°F oven for 2 hours, stirring every 30 minutes.

name implies) instead of rolled. Although they are smaller, steel cut oats are not as thin as rolled oats, so you have to cook them about thirty minutes.

Breakfast can be ready and waiting for you when you wake up if you put oatmeal in a slow cooker attached to an appliance timer when you go to bed. Steel cut oats will benefit from the long soak and will cook faster. Steel cut oats can also be set to soak overnight in a pot of water on the stovetop. When you get up in the morning, you only need to turn on the stove to cook breakfast.

Eggs

If you want a high-protein hot breakfast, eggs may be your answer. They cook incredibly fast. Eggs can be fried, poached, scrambled, or boiled. It only takes five minutes to toast an English muffin, scramble an egg, and put the two together with a slice of cheese for an egg and cheese sandwich. In the middle of a hot summer, eggs can be boiled the night before and kept overnight in the refrigerator to make a tasty breakfast of cold boiled eggs. Eggs also make a fast filling for a breakfast burrito.

Breakfast Burrito

Makes 1 burrito.

1 egg
1 flour tortilla
1-2 ounces cheese, shredded
any of the following options:
  green onions or chives, minced
  red onion, minced
tomato, diced
bacon, fried
sausage, crumbled and fried
hash browns or leftover potatoes,
  diced and fried

Butter a skillet and place it on medium heat. Whisk the egg and pour into skillet, add your choice of optional ingredients and cook until the egg is scrambled. Roll up the cooked ingredients and shredded cheese in a tortilla.

Savings: A breakfast burrito or an English muffin with a scrambled egg and a slice of cheese will save you about $2 compared with a breakfast sandwich at a fast food restaurant.

Pancakes and biscuits

Many people relegate pancakes and biscuits to weekends. But it only takes about ten minutes to get biscuits into the oven. Pancakes are also quick to mix up, but do take time to cook. Fixing pancakes is something that children can learn to do before their teen years, so they can help with the actual cooking. Although you can buy biscuit and pancake mixes in the store, they only save you two or three minutes of preparation time, and they are filled with artificial ingredients. When you compare the cost of homemade to a mix, the homemade is much cheaper.

If you won't eat this many pancakes in one morning, you can make as many as you want and store the remainder of the batter in a covered

Pancakes

Makes about 16 medium-sized pancakes.

2 cups buttermilk or orange juice

2 eggs

2 teaspoons baking powder

1 teaspoon baking soda

½ teaspoon salt

2 cups flour, unbleached, white whole wheat, or a blend

Put all of the ingredients into a bowl and mix with a whisk until the lumps are gone. Butter a skillet or griddle and place it on low to medium heat. Pour ⅓ cup of pancake batter onto the griddle. Turn the pancakes when the bubbles pop and the space doesn't fill in with more liquid batter.

For variety you can add a cup of fresh blueberries or chopped strawberries to the batter before cooking.

container in the refrigerator for two or three days. You can also refrigerate cooked pancakes and reheat them in a pan or a toaster oven.

You can save a few minutes in the morning when making biscuits if you mix up all of the dry ingredients and cut in the butter the night before. Cover the bowl and store it in the refrigerator. When you get up in the morning, turn on the oven, add the buttermilk and roll out the biscuits while the oven heats up.

> **Savings:** A pancake and biscuit mix in my area costs about $1 per pound. If you use non-organic flour, you can make homemade pancakes for half the price. For the same price as the mix, which contains artificial ingredients, you can make pancakes with organic flour.

Biscuits

Makes 16 small biscuits.

2 cups flour, unbleached, white
   whole wheat, or a blend
½ teaspoon salt

2 teaspoons baking powder
¼ cup butter (½ stick)
⅔ cup buttermilk

Put the flour, salt, and baking powder in a bowl and stir. Slice the butter into thin pieces and add to the dry ingredients. Use a pastry blender to cut the butter into the flour mix.

Once the flour has the appearance of coarse cornmeal, add the buttermilk. It will feel like there isn't enough liquid, but don't add more. I usually wind up digging in with my hands and doing the final mixing without a spoon. Once the dough is a well-formed ball, sprinkle a couple tablespoons of flour on a work surface, press the dough ball into the flour, flip over, press into the flour again, and roll it out to about 1-inch thick. Although you can do this on the counter, I prefer to do it on the baking stone or cast iron baking pan that I actually will use for baking the biscuits because it eliminates the need to clean up the countertop afterwards. ☞

A pastry blender makes quick work of combining the butter and flour. If you don't have a pastry blender, you can use two knives to cut the butter into the flour, but the right tool for the job makes it go so much more quickly.

Use a knife to cut the dough into 2-inch squares and space these about an inch apart on a cookie sheet. Bake at 400° F degrees for 15 minutes then turn off the oven to save gas or electricity. Leave the biscuits in the oven with the door closed to continue baking for an additional 5 minutes. Then take them out of the oven and serve.

Although you can use a biscuit cutter to cut the biscuits into pretty little circles, it takes more time. You have to keep reworking the leftover dough because there are a lot of scraps when you cut out circles, and, really, the only reason for doing it is cosmetic. The speckles in these biscuits are minced green onions.

Garlic and cheddar biscuit variation — use only 2 tablespoons of butter, add ½ cup shredded cheddar cheese and 1 teaspoon garlic powder before adding the buttermilk.

Onion or chive biscuit variation — Add 2 tablespoons of minced red onion, minced chives, or minced green onions before adding the buttermilk.

What's white whole wheat flour? Most of the flour sold in the store as "whole wheat" comes from red wheat, which has a strong taste and makes breads and pastries that are heavy in texture. White wheat is a different plant. White whole wheat flour is lighter in color, has a milder flavor, and creates breads and pastries that are lighter in texture. If your family is not accustomed to whole grains, introduce it to them starting with a blend that is three-fourths unbleached and one-fourth white whole wheat. Gradually increase the proportion of whole wheat in recipes as they become accustomed to it.

> **Savings:** A garlic cheddar biscuit mix costs about $1.50 and makes only six biscuits. These homemade biscuits cost less than 10 cents each to make from scratch using organic flour, for a savings of 90 cents for six biscuits.

Yogurt

One of my favorite breakfasts in the middle of summer is a smoothie made with yogurt and fresh fruit. It takes only a couple of minutes to mix up everything in the blender. If you're in a hurry, you can drink it while you're running around the house getting ready for your day. Of course, you should sit down to enjoy your meals in a relaxed environment, but on those days when you're rushed, this is a good alternative to skipping breakfast or hitting the drive-through of a fast food restaurant. I also love to eat fresh yogurt with granola.

Making yogurt is easy, and the savings can add up for those who eat yogurt regularly because a quart of milk costs less than a quart of yogurt, and the cost of a starter is negligible. Although there are a lot of online recipes that suggest using yogurt from the store as your starter, I recommend using a commercial yogurt starter because it will yield more predictable results. Store-bought yogurt may not always have live cultures at the time you buy it. A little of your homemade yogurt can be used as a starter for the next batch. You can make your own fruit flavored yogurt by adding jam when serving.

> **Savings:** Subtract the cost of a quart of milk from a quart of yogurt in your area to figure out how much you will save by making your own yogurt.

Lunches and Dinners

Eating out, especially at fast food restaurants, is the opposite of eco-thrifty, and frozen dinners are not much better, although you may feel like you have no choice if you work outside the home. Even if you want to eat something as simple as a sandwich for lunch, making it at home and putting it into a reusable container to take to work is cheaper and greener than buying a sandwich in a restaurant. You can also prepare a variety of pasta salads or potato salad to take to work for lunch. It is even easier to avoid eating out for dinner because the meal does not usually need to be portable.

Although there are recipes in this section, this is not like a typical cookbook. Rather than giving you dozens of recipes that have to be followed to the letter, I'm giving you a few flexible recipes along with the information you need to be able to cook a variety of meals, using what you have in your kitchen. You will be able to save time and money while eating healthier foods.

Beans

Beans are a misunderstood and maligned food. They are perfectly wonderful once you know how to cook with them. Although they take a long time to cook, they require very little attention, which means they actually take very little of your time. The variety of dried beans is astonishing with dozens from which to choose. Some are strongly associated with various ethnic cuisines, such as pinto and black beans with Mexican food and lentils and garbanzo beans with Indian cuisine. Many can simply be cooked with a few spices and a little salt for a very easy dinner. Others can be added to soups, such as chili and minestrone. Beans can be used for lunches or dinners, as a side dish, main dish, or snack.

Although a can of beans seems to be cheap enough, usually costing a dollar or less, you can save about 75 percent if you cook dried beans. To make life even more convenient, cook large amounts of beans and then freeze them for quick meals later. And cooking beans is an easy process:

1. Pour the desired amount (based on the recipe or how you plan to use them) onto a flat surface and sort through the beans to make sure there are no little dirt clods or stones that passed through the harvesting equipment.
2. Rinse the beans in a colander. Put them in a pot.
3. Cover the beans with water and add the same amount of water so that if the beans are two inches deep in the pot, you'll have four inches of water in the pot.

    To save time and money, buy beans in bulk and cook as many as you can at one time. Using your largest pot, fill it one-third full of beans, then two-thirds full of water.
4. Soak the beans as needed. While the larger beans, such as kidney and garbanzo beans, need to be soaked overnight to shorten the cooking time, smaller legumes, such as split peas and lentils, can be cooked in less than an hour without soaking.

    If the beans require soaking, you can soak them overnight, or if you need them sooner, bring the water to a boil, turn off the heat, cover the pot, and let the beans sit in the hot water for two or three hours.
5. Cook the beans in enough water to cover them by two inches. You may need to add water if the level has dropped during soaking. Cook covered over a low heat until done. If your stove burner cannot be turned down low enough to keep the pot from boiling over, you may need to tip the lid to let steam escape.

    Cooking times for beans will depend on a few factors. The larger the bean, the longer it takes to cook. Smaller beans, such as pintos or black beans, will only take one or two hours to cook. Larger beans,

like kidneys and garbanzos, may take closer to three hours. The older
the beans, the more they have dried out and the longer they will take

White Bean Spread

Makes filling for 4 sandwiches.

2 cups cooked white beans
  (navy or great northern)
1 small onion, chopped
2 tablespoons oil

1 clove garlic, crushed
1 red bell pepper, chopped
1 tablespoon soy sauce (optional)

Sauté the onion and red pepper in oil until the onion is transparent. Mash the
beans and garlic in a food processor or in a bowl. Add the onion and red pepper,
and mix until thoroughly combined. Add soy sauce, if you like it. Add salt and pepper to taste. This spread tastes best if served chilled. The spread can be stored
in the refrigerator for three or four days before the taste starts to change in an
unpleasant direction. You can freeze it for longer term storage.

Red Bean Spread

Makes filling for 4 sandwiches.

2 cups cooked red beans
  (kidney, small red, cranberry)
½ onion, chopped
2 cloves garlic, crushed
1 tomato, chopped

1 tablespoon chili powder
½ teaspoon paprika
½ teaspoon salt
⅛ teaspoon black pepper

Put all the ingredients into a food processor and blend until the spread is a
smooth consistency. It really is important to chop the onion before putting it
into the food processor because otherwise you will probably have some large
onion chunks in the finished spread. This spread makes a nice bean dip for snacking with tortilla chips. It can be stored in the refrigerator for a few days or in the
freezer for long-term storage

to cook. Beans will also take more time to cook in hard water or when salt or tomato sauce is added to the pot before the beans are cooked.

Cook beans in large quantities and store them in the freezer in various sized containers, based upon their intended use. For example, I store pinto beans, which will be used in burritos or the Tamale Pie recipe,

Tamale Pie

Makes 8 servings.

4 cups cooked pinto or kidney beans
1 onion, chopped
2 tomatoes, chopped
1 green pepper, chopped
1 cup corn kernels
2 cups tomato sauce
2 to 4 tablespoons chili powder (I like a lot)

1 teaspoon salt
½ teaspoon black pepper
2 cups cheddar cheese, shredded
Green onion or chives (optional)
cornbread batter (recipe follows)
1 teaspoon cumin

Grease and flour a pie pan. Mix up the cornbread recipe and pour the batter into the pie pan. Mix together the rest of the ingredients except for the cheddar cheese, and pour the mix on top of the cornbread batter. Bake at 350°F for 30 minutes. Turn off the oven; remove pie from oven. Sprinkle shredded cheddar over the top and return it to the oven. Let the residual heat melt the cheddar. I like to snip a fresh from the garden green onion or chives over the top before serving.

Cornbread

1 cup cornmeal
1 cup flour
2 teaspoons baking powder
½ teaspoon salt

1 tablespoon sugar
1 cup milk
¼ cup oil or melted butter

Mix the dry ingredients together in a bowl and then add the milk and oil and stir to thoroughly combine everything.

in four-cup containers. I store cooked white and red beans for making spreads in two-cup containers. When I'm planning to use black beans in a Mexican bean casserole, I store them in a seven-cup container.

One reason I cook beans in bulk and freeze them is so that I can toss together a meal quickly. If I'm looking ahead towards a busy day, I pull a four-cup container of frozen beans out of the freezer to thaw. In the afternoon, I can put this nutritious casserole together in about ten minutes and put it in the oven to cook while I continue with my life.

Bread

Making yeast bread seems to be scarier than making any other food. Many accomplished cooks won't even try it. It has a reputation for being time-consuming and difficult. Neither is true. Most of the time involved in its preparation is time that it sits alone, unattended, on your counter. As for difficulty, the whole thing will be demystified for you in the next few pages, and you will see how simple it is. Although entire books are written on bread, a great deal of the content of those books is repeated information. There are really only three basic bread recipes, and from these, you can make dozens of different types of bread.

French bread is the simplest with only four ingredients: water, flour, salt, and yeast. It is also the lowest calorie count because it has no sugar or oil. You cannot use whole grains for French bread. The lack of sugar in the recipe means the yeast has little to feed on and doesn't expand a lot, which would lighten the dough. A whole grain dough, then, is too heavy to rise much.

Basic bread dough has six ingredients, including a small amount of sweetener (sugar, honey, or maple syrup) and fat (oil or butter). You can use a wide variety of liquids with this recipe, depending on whether you want bread for breakfast, dinner, or snacking. Flavors and textures can be created by adding different ingredients. Whole grains work well with this recipe and will produce a stretchy loaf of bread using as much as two-thirds whole grains. Because there are no preservatives, homemade bread will dry out within a couple days, but stale bread makes great poultry stuffing or croutons.

Croutons

Cube the bread, sprinkle with garlic salt, and spread in a single layer on an oiled cookie sheet. Bake in a 200°F oven for 2 hours.

The third type of dough is for sweet breads, and it is the highest calorie bread because it contains a large amount of butter and sugar or honey, as well as eggs.

The following recipes all make one loaf or about a dozen rolls, which is what a standard bread machine will hold. Double the recipe for a stand mixer with a four- or five-quart bowl. Triple the recipe for a six-quart bowl or larger, making three loaves or three-dozen rolls. As you double and triple the recipe, you need proportionally less flour. In other words, if one loaf requires three cups of flour, three loaves may require only eight cups. If that sounds scary, don't worry. I'll explain what you need to know to make this work.

It does not take any longer to mix up two or three loaves than it does to mix up one loaf, so it makes sense to mix up as many as your bowl will accommodate. When mixing by hand, you can mix up five or six loaves at once with a big enough bowl. Bake multiple loaves at one time, and freeze the extra loaves for future use. For fresh, hot bread daily, bake one loaf at a time and store the rest of the dough in an oiled bowl loosely covered in the refrigerator. When you put a ball of dough into an oiled bowl for storage, roll the dough around so that it becomes coated with a thin layer of oil and won't stick to the bowl or the cover. Let the dough warm up to room temperature for a couple of hours before baking it. You can bake it sooner, but you won't get as high a rise from the bread if it hasn't been able to warm up before being put into the oven.

Basic steps

The basic method for making bread does not vary much from one type to another. Most bread recipes give very specific information, such as an exact temperature for the water and an exact amount of time for rising.

But I find this type of information simply sets people up to fail. I've heard many people say that they can't bake bread because the house isn't warm enough. In reality, they simply did not let the dough rise long enough. If your house is 65°F, it will take longer for your bread to rise than if it is 80°F. Rather than giving you a list of rules to follow, the goal here is to educate you about how yeast works and how you can work with it.

1. Start by putting the warm liquid into the bowl. You can use a thermometer to make sure it is 100°F, but basically, the temperature needs to be the same as for a nice bath, so usually you have the correct temperature if you use tap water that is comfortably warm. Sprinkle the yeast on top of the water.

2. Add all of the other ingredients except the flour.

3. Once everything is in the bowl, add two-thirds of the flour to the bowl and stir until thoroughly mixed. If you are doing this by hand (rather than with a stand mixer and dough hook), you will probably need to toss the spoon and dig in with your hands. Add the remaining flour slowly, a quarter cup at a time, mixing until the dough forms a nice ball that does not stick to the sides of the bowl or to your fingers. It is important that you thoroughly mix the ingredients after each addition of flour before adding more flour. It is quite easy to add more flour, but if you wind up with dough that is too dry, it is a messy proposition to add more liquid. In most cases, you won't use the maximum amount of flour listed, but feel free to add more flour if the dough is still sticky.

4. Although you will have a lighter, airier loaf of bread if you let it rise two or more times, bread can be baked on a single rise. If you are in a hurry, you can pull out a piece of dough, put it into a bread pan, let it rise for 30 minutes and bake it. You can also make pizza, rolls, or flatbread with dough on the first rise. If you have time to let the dough rise in the mixing bowl for at least 30 minutes, you will be rewarded by stretchier dough that is easier to roll out or knead and shape into a loaf or rolls. If you forget about your dough, and it rises in the bowl for several hours, it's not a big deal. Punch it down and

If the bread dough looks shiny and wet and sticks to the bowl, the dough hook, or your fingers, it needs more flour. Add another ¼ cup and mix for another two or three minutes to thoroughly combine ingredients.

Some people might look at this dough and think it is ready for the next step because it looks like it has formed into a ball. However, it is too early to decide whether it is ready because there is still flour in the bowl that needs to be mixed in. This dough actually was still too wet and needed more flour.

put it in the bread pan. Let it rise for about 30 minutes. If it over-rises in the bread pan and has tripled or more in size, you will probably want to punch it down and let it rise again. Although you can bake bread that has risen too high, there will be big bubbles inside the loaf, so the bread won't be as pretty as you might like. The large air bubbles will make it difficult for the bread to hold together, and it will tend to crumble and fall apart. (Crumbly bread can be used for bread pudding or stuffing poultry and can be frozen until needed.) The main thing to remember is that you don't need to stress about following instructions exactly with bread. It's sad that so many people think

If the bread dough looks flaky and you see a lot of flour in the bowl, continue mixing for a couple more minutes to be sure everything is thoroughly combined before deciding you have too much flour. This picture was taken only two minutes before the next one where the bread is perfect.

The bread dough is ready! It has formed a nice ball that is pushed around the bowl by the dough hook. It doesn't stick to the bowl or the dough hook, and if you press your fingers into it, the dough doesn't stick to your fingers either. It is ready for rising!

bread is persnickety because it is actually quite forgiving once you understand it — kind of like some people.

5. Bake the dough for the amount of time specified in the recipe and check the loaf by thumping it with your finger. If it sounds hollow, it's done. If you're new to baking bread and the concept of "hollow sounding" is elusive, you can use a thermometer. The loaf is done when it reaches 200°F internally. Color is also a good indicator when making bread with unbleached flour. When baking the bread at the temperatures suggested, it is unlikely to be cooked thoroughly if it is not a lovely golden brown. It is a bit more challenging to use color for

determining when bread is done when using whole grains. Because the dough is darker from the beginning, it is easy to think it's done before it is baked throughout.

I prefer stoneware or cast iron to glass, aluminum, or stainless steel pans for baking bread and rolls. Stoneware and cast iron create a bottom crust that matches the top and sides in color and level of doneness. If you use glass or lightweight metal bread pans, decrease the temperature in the recipes by 25 degrees.

French bread

You can use this recipe to make baguettes, hoagie-style sandwich rolls, hamburger buns, flat bread, and dinner rolls.

We use flat bread to make sandwiches or hamburgers or as an accompaniment to Indian foods.

French Bread

Makes 1 baguette or 6 to 8 sandwich rolls, hamburger buns, or flatbreads, or 1 dozen dinner rolls.

1 cup warm water
½ tablespoon yeast
1 teaspoon salt

2 ½ cups unbleached flour
1 tablespoon oil

Combine all ingredients except oil and mix the dough according to the instructions that begin on page 80 and let rise once in the mixing bowl. Pour 1 tablespoon of oil onto a baking sheet and rub it across the surface with your fingers. Rub excess oil into your hands to make the dough easier to handle. Shape the dough into baguettes or dinner rolls and place them on the oiled baking sheet, leaving a couple of inches between each one. Let rise 20 to 30 minutes. Spritz with water for an extra crunchy crust, and bake at 400°F for 20 to 25 minutes.

Hamburger buns: Divide the dough into eight equal sized pieces, and roll each piece into a thin circle about 2½ to 3 inches across. The challenge in making a hamburger bun is simply making it small enough so that it won't be too big to fit into your mouth after the dough has risen and expanded the size of the bun.

Basic bread

The recipe that we make most often is the basic bread recipe, which works well for pizza dough, dinner rolls, and sandwich bread.

Basic Bread

Makes 1 loaf or 1 dozen rolls

1 cup liquid*

½ tablespoon yeast

2 tablespoons oil or softened butter

2 tablespoons sugar or honey

1 teaspoon salt

3 cups flour

optional ingredients**

Mix the dough according to the steps on page 80, let it rise once and punch down. Shape it into a loaf and place into an oiled bread pan or shape the dough into rolls and place on an oiled baking sheet or in an oiled muffin pan. Let rise about 30 minutes. Bake a loaf of bread at 350°F for 40 to 45 minutes. Bake rolls at 350°F for 25 to 30 minutes.

*You can use water, milk, juice, whey, or water in which potatoes were boiled. Milk makes the dough a little heavier and adds protein to the bread. Juice can be added for flavor. Orange juice makes great breakfast bread. Tomato juice makes a tasty bread to serve with salad. Whey is a natural dough conditioner and is great for helping whole grain breads to rise. The starch in potato water also helps to create a lighter loaf of bread.

**Optional ingredients can include ½ cup of rolled oats, raisins, or chopped nuts or two tablespoons of flax seeds. A tablespoon of dried basil makes a nice addition when using tomato juice as the liquid. A half cup of dried cranberries goes well with orange juice as the liquid.

Bread machines

You can make the basic bread and sweet bread recipes in a bread machine. Use the full amount of flour in each recipe. If the dough seems dry, use 2 tablespoons less flour next time.

Flat Bread

Makes 6 to 8 pieces.

French bread dough or basic bread dough for 1 loaf
oil for skillet or griddle

Let the dough rise for 30 minutes. Pull off a ball about the size of a large egg, and roll it into a flat circle about 6 to 8 inches across. Brown one side for a couple minutes on a hot oiled griddle until bubbles start to rise up in the bread. Then flip it and brown the other side for a couple of minutes.

Sweet bread

You can use this dough to make brioche and cinnamon rolls. It also makes a delicious loaf of bread that can be eaten plain or used for French toast or bread pudding.

Sweet Bread

Makes 1 loaf or 1 dozen rolls

½ cup water
½ tablespoon yeast
1 teaspoon salt
½ cup butter (1 stick)
3 tablespoons honey
3 eggs
3½ cups flour

Mix the dough according to the steps on page 98, let it rise once and punch it down. Shape dough and place into an oiled bread pan or shape into rolls and place on an oiled baking sheet or in an oiled muffin pan.

To make crescent shaped dinner rolls roll out the dough into a 12-inch circle. Use a pizza cutter or large knife to cut the dough into twelve triangles.

To form the rolls, begin rolling up the triangle from the smallest side. Make sure the tip is tucked under the roll when you place it on the pan, or it will pop up when baking.

Cinnamon Rolls

Makes 1 dozen rolls.

sweet bread dough for 1 loaf
2 tablespoons butter at
   room temperature

¼ cup of granulated sugar
1 tablespoon of cinnamon

Roll out the dough in a rectangle 12 inches long. Spread 2 tablespoons of room-temperature butter on the dough, and then sprinkle ¼ cup of sugar and 2 tablespoons of cinnamon on the dough. ☞

Roll the dough into a 18-inch long log by lifting the longer edge first.

Slice the roll every inch to make twelve ½-inch rolls. Cutting with a knife usually smashes the dough and the cinnamon rolls are not very round. Using cotton thread or unwaxed dental floss, slide the thread under the roll and lift.

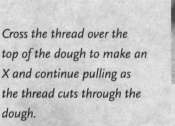

Cross the thread over the top of the dough to make an X and continue pulling as the thread cuts through the dough.

Place the sliced cinnamon rolls 2 inches apart on an oiled baking sheet. Let them rise 20 to 30 minutes. Bake the rolls at 350°F degrees for 20 to 25 minutes. Add frosting if you like.

> **Savings:** Although bread may not seem expensive at $2- $4 a loaf in the grocery store, you can make the French bread and basic bread recipe for about $1 a loaf using organic ingredients.

Sandwiches

Luncheon meat was one of the first things I cut out of my diet when I started to learn about nutrition. Cured meats contain sodium nitrates and nitrites, which have been associated with stomach cancer. They also tend to be high in fat and salt and low in protein and nutrition. And when you do the math, processed meat is expensive per pound, especially when you realize how little nutrition it contains.

American cheese is not cheese, and it is not as nutritious as real cheese, such as cheddar or gouda. It contains a lot of ingredients, including emulsifiers and preservatives, that you don't find in real cheese. The label usually says it is a processed "cheese food" or a processed "cheese product." You may even see some labeled as Swiss or mozzarella, along with the word "processed," which means it is not a true cheese. Processed cheese tends to be softer than real cheese, and it is often sold in a can, a plastic container, or individually sliced and wrapped. Like most processed foods, it is cheap but not especially nutritious.

Natural peanut butter, which is high in protein and inexpensive, can be part of an ecothrifty sandwich, but read the label to make sure the peanut butter does not contain partially hydrogenated oils. When made from real peanuts, the oil will separate as the peanut butter sits on the shelf, which is why many companies remove the natural peanut oil and mix partially hydrogenated oil back into the spread. Partially hydrogenated oil contains trans fat, which leads to circulatory problems and heart disease.

The least expensive and most nutritious sandwiches are those that simply contain real food, such as sliced meat (turkey, chicken, beef, pork), real cheese, natural peanut butter, vegetables, and beans. Choice of bread is also important. I usually prefer sandwiches on a roll made from my French bread recipe, but for a change, I enjoy sandwiches on flat bread, wrapped up in a tortilla, or stuffed in a pita. Homemade bread baked in a traditional loaf pan is especially good for sandwiches when it is a day old. When making sandwiches to take to work or school, be mindful of the fact that you won't be eating it for a few hours and don't include ingredients that will turn the bread soggy, such as tomato slices.

Sandwich Suggestions:

- Avocado slices, alfalfa sprouts, crushed garlic, sliced cheddar
- Grilled button mushrooms, sweet bell peppers of various colors, caramelized onions, and goat cheese or brie
- Grilled Portobello mushrooms and goat cheese
- Mozzarella, sliced tomatoes, and pesto or fresh basil
- Red bean spread with shredded cheddar cheese (page 77)
- Sliced meat, lettuce, and tomato with garlic mayonnaise
- White bean spread with alfalfa sprouts (page 77)

> **Savings:** A sandwich at a national chain restaurant in my area costs $5-$7, compared with a homemade sandwich, which costs less than $1 per person.

Casseroles

Like pasta salads, you can make an endless variety of casseroles by simply switching around ingredients in the standard casserole formula. For a main dish casserole, you need a protein source, a sauce, a starch, and some vegetables. Protein sources can be any type of meat, cheese, or beans. The starch can be rice, pasta, potatoes, or breadcrumbs. The sauce can be a cream soup, a tomato soup, or salsa. And the vegetables can be whatever complements the rest of the ingredients.

Pasta salads

Pasta salads are quick and easy, and depending on the ingredients, they can be a main dish or a side. Really, the only difference between the two is that a pasta salad as a main dish includes a protein source, such as meat, cheese, or beans. If you are in a hurry and don't have all of the

Shepherd's Pie

Serves 4.

1 pound ground lamb, browned
1 cup peas and sliced carrots, steamed
2 cups cream soup (half of the recipe on page 96)
1 pound potatoes, cooked and mashed

Put the ground lamb in a deep dish pie plate and add the peas and carrots evenly. Pour the cream soup over everything, and top with mashed potatoes.

Because all of the ingredients are already cooked or need only minimal cooking in the casserole, 30 minutes in a 350°F oven will take care of it. The idea is to brown the mashed potatoes a bit.

Although lamb is traditional in Shepherd's Pie, you can substitute ground beef as a thrifty option.

Broccoli Cheddar Casserole

Serves 4.

3 cups Cheddar Broccoli Soup (half a batch of the recipe on page 96)
4 cups cooked rice
1 cup shredded cheddar

Mix the soup and rice and spread into a 2-quart casserole pan. Sprinkle the cheddar on top. If you are starting with hot ingredients, bake at 350 degrees for 20 minutes. When using cold leftovers straight from the refrigerator, bake for 30 minutes.

Main dish option: Mix in a can of tuna fish before baking to turn this into a main dish casserole.

Green Bean Casserole

Serves 4 to 6.

3 cups Cream of Mushroom Soup (half of the recipe on page 96)
1 pound green beans, steamed
1 onion, chopped
1 tablespoon butter

Place the green beans in a 2-quart casserole dish and pour the mushroom soup over the beans. Melt the butter in a saucepan and brown the chopped onion over low heat until it is carmelized. Sprinkle the onion evenly over the green beans and bake in a 350°F oven for 25 minutes.

Halving and Doubling Recipes

There are times when you want to prepare a recipe but you need a bigger or a smaller quantity than the recipe makes. For example, some of the casserole recipes in this book call for half of a cream soup recipe and there are times when I like to double a recipe so we will have lots of leftovers, especially when making soups and casseroles. It takes no longer to make twice as much. In most cases, it is easy to change the number of servings simply by multiplying or dividing the ingredients.

ingredients for one of your tried-and-true meals, you can improvise with a pasta salad or a casserole. For a pasta salad side dish, you only need one pound of uncooked pasta, two to four tablespoons of sauce, and something colorful, which usually means vegetables. Add a protein source like chopped chicken, tuna, or tofu to make a main dish.

Here are some ideas for pasta salad combinations. The ingredients can be recombined to suit your preferences.

- Bow-tie pasta, Italian salad dressing, sliced zucchini, black olives
- Elbow macaroni, mayonnaise, canned tuna fish, green peas

- Penne, pesto, mozzarella cheese cubes, diced tomatoes
- Rotini, mayonnaise, dill, garlic, sliced zucchini, shredded carrots
- Ziti, mayonnaise, chopped chicken, pineapple cubes, chopped red onions, parsley

Potatoes

When my children were small, baked potatoes were one of their favorite lunches. Far from merely being a supporting player in a steak dinner, a potato can take the stage as the star of the meal. They are especially good at dressing up leftovers. When we have leftover chili, we love to bake potatoes, cut them open, smother them with the chili, sprinkle some shredded cheddar cheese on top, and add a dollop of plain yogurt or sour cream, and snipped green onions when they're in season. If you happen to have some salsa in the refrigerator, add a tablespoonful or two to your potato.

A cold baked potato can also be the palette on which you create a salad. Cut the potato in half lengthwise, then in fourths lengthwise, and place the pieces on the plate skin down. Top with small cubes of cheddar cheese and fresh-shelled peas, and drizzle with a tablespoon or two of mayonnaise dressing.

Leftover steamed broccoli from last night's dinner goes well served with cheddar cheese on a baked potato. Leftover chicken and gravy is also a tasty addition to a baked potato.

Our baked potatoes are tastier than most, and my method for preparing them also makes for especially soft hands. Yes, you read that correctly. You will get tasty spuds and soft hands. If you are baking four potatoes, measure out ¼ cup of oil and add 2 tablespoons of salt to the oil. Stir it up and fill the palm of one cupped hand with the mix. Pick up the potato and rub the mixture all over it, then place it on the baking sheet. Repeat the process with the other potatoes. After placing the last potato on the baking sheet, rub your hands together and rub the salt and oil mixture onto the backs of your hands and between your fingers. Wash your hands with soap and pat dry. Grape seed oil works especially well for this because it is excellent for your skin and it handles the high heat in the oven, but sunflower oil is also a good choice. Although olive oil is great for your skin, it smokes at high temperatures, so it is not a good option for baking potatoes. Bake medium potatoes at 400°F for 60 minutes, large potatoes for 75 minutes, or until fork easily pierces the potatoes.

Soups

For years, split pea soup was one of our favorite dinners in the winter. When I worked full time, I would start the soup in a slow cooker and put dough ingredients in the bread maker before leaving in the morning. We would arrive home in the evening to the wonderful aroma of fresh bread and split pea soup. For those who think split pea soup is boring, or if you are a fan of spicy food, try adding a few drops of hot sauce to this soup.

If you know that your slow cooker can cook split peas in less time than you'll be gone, use an appliance timer to start the cooking in time for the soup to be ready when you get home from work. It is usually best to try this first on a day when you will be home to watch the cooking in progress so that you don't undercook the split peas or wind up with a pot that is completely dried out and a big pain to clean.

Split Pea Soup

Serves 4.

2 cups dried split peas

2 quarts water

½ cup dried great northern beans
 or navy beans

¼ cup barley

1 onion, chopped

2 carrots, sliced

2 stalks celery, sliced

1 medium potato, peeled and chopped

½ teaspoon celery seed

¼ to 1 teaspoon black pepper

½ teaspoon salt

Put all of the ingredients into a pot and cook over low heat for about 2 hours. Watch it very closely towards the end because as the peas cook, they can start to stick and burn. I prefer to use a slow cooker for this soup because it cooks on such a low, even heat, I don't have to worry about burning.

This soup makes a satisfying, nutritious, and frugal meal served with grilled cheese sandwiches made with slices of cheddar cheese and whole grain bread made from the basic bread recipe.

Minestrone is another great soup to make on a day when you can't spend much time in the kitchen. It also works well in a slow cooker. If you will be gone all day, don't add the pasta until you get home because it will be cooked to pieces after a few hours.

Once you know how to make a cream sauce, you can make virtually any type of cream soup. In addition to being able to make all kinds of soup, you will also be able to replace those cans of cream soups used in casseroles. Like a lot of foods, they seem cheap, but their homemade

Minestrone Soup

Serves 4.

2 cups dried kidney beans, soaked for 4 hours or overnight	1 pound chopped tomatoes, frozen or canned
2 quarts water	½ teaspoon dried marjoram
1 onion, chopped	1 teaspoon dried basil
4 cloves garlic, crushed	1 tablespoon dried oregano
2 stalks celery, sliced	½ teaspoon black pepper
2 carrots, sliced	1 teaspoon salt
2 medium potatoes, cubed	1 cup uncooked rotini or penne pasta
½ pound green beans, sliced	

Drain the soaking beans and put them in a 5-quart pot. Add the 2 quarts of water. Cook over low heat until the beans are almost done, which will take about 2 hours. Add the rest of the ingredients to the pot except for the pasta. Cook for 30 minutes, add the pasta and cook until it is done. If you have any spinach or cabbage in the refrigerator, feel free to add a cup to the pot.

Alternatively, put all the ingredients except the pasta in a slow cooker and cook on low for 6 to 8 hours. Then add the pasta and cook until the pasta is done.

Cream Soup Base

Makes 4 servings.

¼ cup butter (½ stick)
¼ cup flour
4 cups milk

½ teaspoon salt
¼ teaspoon pepper
white wine (if desired)

Melt the butter in a pot over low heat so you don't scorch it. Whisk the flour into the melted butter and continue to stir until all lumps have disappeared. Add the milk, turn up the heat to medium, and continue stirring until the mixture bubbles. Turn off the heat, add salt and pepper, and add a splash of white wine, if you like.

counterpart costs a fraction of the price, and there are no cans left to be recycled or to go to the landfill.

You can turn this soup base into any of the cream soups below by adding the listed ingredients.

- Cream of mushroom: Add 8 ounces of sliced mushrooms, browned in 2 tablespoons of butter. A splash of leftover red wine goes especially well in mushroom soup.
- Cream of broccoli: Add 4 cups chopped broccoli, steamed.
- Cheddar broccoli: Add 1 cup shredded cheddar while stirring constantly, then add 4 cups chopped broccoli, steamed.
- Cream of spinach: Add 4 cups chopped, raw spinach.
- Corn chowder: Add 1 pound of corn kernels, 1 red pepper, chopped, and 2 small potatoes, peeled, cubed, and browned in 2 tablespoons oil.
- Cream of chicken or turkey: Add 1 cup of cubed, cooked chicken or turkey, and 1 cup of cooked rice.

You can add a chopped onion to any of the soups by sautéing it in the butter for a few minutes before adding the flour.

Stretching meat

If you search for "rubber chicken" online, you will get lots of links to sites that sell the rubber chickens used for gags, but add the word "recipe" to your search, and you will learn how to stretch a chicken for several meals. The concept has been around for many years. Depending on the size of your family and the size of the chickens, you can start with one or more whole chickens and either roast or stew the meat initially. Because we raise our own chickens, I like to start with one or two stew hens, which are three years old and are not laying a lot of eggs any longer. Chickens of that age should be cooked in water over a low heat for several hours. If you buy eggs directly from a farmer, let them know that you'd like to buy stew hens whenever they decide to butcher their old layers. Store-bought chicken, which is quite young and tender, starts with roasting. Here are a couple of different rubber chicken menus.

Young Chicken (grocery store chicken)

Day 1   Roast Chicken: Roast the chicken in the oven surrounded by potatoes, onions, carrots, and celery. Store the leftover chicken in the refrigerator.

Day 2   Soup: Strip all meat from the bones and return the meat to the refrigerator. Put the bones in a pot and cover with water. Simmer for two or three hours to make a broth. Remove the bones and use the broth to make a lentil soup or add vegetables and noodles or rice for a soup.

Day 3   Casserole: Chop the leftover meat and use it in a casserole, as described in the casserole section.

Day 4   If you have enough meat for additional meals, you can make chicken salad, chicken sandwich spread (page 98), or another casserole.

Older Chicken (stew hen)

Day 1   Soup: Put the chicken, two carrots, sliced, two stalks of celery, sliced, and one onion, chopped, in a pot of water and simmer for several hours until you can pull the meat off the bones with a fork. Remove the chicken from the pot and allow it to cool on a platter. Pull the meat off the bones, chop it into bite-sized pieces, and store it in the refrigerator. Older hens tend to have a lot of fat on them, which will float on the top of the water. Skim this fat off and store it in the refrigerator. When refrigerated, it will become solid like lard or vegetable shortening. For true chicken gravy, use the chicken fat instead of butter in a gravy recipe. Pour half of the broth in a jar and store it in the refrigerator. Use the remaining broth to make lentil soup or add noodles or rice.

Day 2   Casserole: Use some of the chopped chicken to make a casserole.

Day 3   Chicken and dumplings: Use the reserved broth and a cup of the chicken to make chicken and dumplings.

Day 4   Use the same options listed in the first menu.

The main difference between using a young chicken and an older chicken is that the older chicken will make a much richer broth, which can be stretched farther, and you will have the fat for using later in gravy. The concept of the expandable chicken can also be used with a turkey. Although many people do this for Thanksgiving, the concept works equally well the rest of the year. If your family does not typically eat the legs and thighs on Thanksgiving or Christmas, you can cut them off and use them later to make soup as in the second chicken example. Because

Chicken Salad Spread

Makes 4 sandwiches.

½ cup mayonnaise
1 green onion, snipped into small pieces
juice of half a lemon
2 cups cooked chicken, cubed

1 cup celery, chopped
1 tablespoon dried parsley
½ teaspoon salt
¼ teaspoon pepper

Mix all the ingredients together in a bowl until blended thoroughly. This is excellent on a French bread roll or in a pita.

turkey legs and thighs are dark meat, they work especially well with recipes that you would normally make with beef or pork, such as stroganoff. This concept can also work with ham, beef roasts, and leg of lamb.

> **Savings:** Considering the fact that eating dinner in a restaurant usually costs $10 to $30 per person, and most of these home-cooked meals cost $10 or less for four servings, it is easy to see that you can reduce your food costs by 80 to 90 percent by eating out less often.

Sweets and Treats

Recent research has revealed some scary facts about our eating habits. Basically, snacking plays a large role in many of our health and weight problems. Although we could debate the issue, the fact is that we do snack too much, and we snack on things that are usually empty calories. A piece of cake or a few potato chips every now and then never hurt anyone. However, if we are eating these things daily — or more often — our health will suffer. Like most people, I do enjoy sweets and snack foods, but only eating what I have time to prepare from scratch naturally limits how often we eat those foods.

Desserts

Cakes, cookies, and pastries may be the hardest food items to pass up in the grocery store. They are just sitting there, looking tasty and ready to eat. However, by now you know what I'm going to say. You can make it cheaper at home, and it will taste better and be better for you. Although desserts sold in grocery store bakeries may have been baked recently, they are usually made from mixes, which means they contain chemical additives, and you know that bright blue icing is artificially colored.

The fact that most of us don't have a lot of time to make desserts at home is a good thing. We should not be eating them every day. Even if you make dessert with natural ingredients, it still is not one of the food groups required for sustenance. Over the years I have learned a few tricks that make it easy for us to have home-baked treats a couple of times a week. For starters, if you have children, teach them to bake their favorite desserts. If they are like my children were, they will be more than happy to learn to bake if it means they will be having more sweets around the house.

Cookies take more time than almost anything else because each one has to be placed on the baking sheet and cooked. It usually takes three or four pans to bake an entire batch, meaning that you are tied to the kitchen for forty-five minutes or longer. I rarely bake drop or rolled cookies. Instead, I bake cakes, pies, and bar cookies, which are cooked in a single pan all at once like a cake, and are then cut into squares. Brownies are probably the most famous bar cookie, but you can turn almost any drop cookie recipe into a bar cookie.

You are probably wondering why pies are included. Don't they take a lot of time, especially with pie crusts? As much as I love a good pie crust, I don't like making them, so I've come up with a variety of pies that don't use a crust.

Berry Custard Pie

Makes one 9-inch pie.

2 cups fresh berries
2 eggs
1 cup milk

¼ cup sugar
¼ cup flour

Butter a pie dish and scatter the berries evenly in the pan. Put the rest of the ingredients into a blender and blend until well mixed and then pour the custard mix over the berries. Sprinkle a tablespoon of sugar over the top if desired. Bake at 350°F for 40 minutes or until a knife makes a clean cut in the pie.

This recipe can be varied to make an apple custard or a pear custard pie. Follow the directions for the Berry Custard Pie substituting apple or pear slices for the berries and adding 1 teaspoon vanilla to the custard mix in the blender before mixing. For the apple pie, sprinkle cinnamon on top of the custard mix before baking.

Raspberry Pear Crisp

Makes 9 servings.

4 pears, peeled and cut into
    one-inch pieces
1 cup raspberries
¾ cup flour

¾ cup rolled oats
¾ cup brown sugar
¼ cup butter (½ stick)

Put the pears in a 9 x 9-inch baking dish and evenly scatter the raspberries over them. In a bowl, use a pastry blender to cut the butter into the flour, oats, and brown sugar. When the mixture is the consistency of coarse cornmeal through-out, sprinkle it on top of the fruit. Bake at 375°F for 30 minutes.

Bar cookies

Many cookie recipes can be turned into bar cookies by simply spreading the cookie dough evenly into a bar pan, which is similar to a cookie sheet but has one-inch high sides. Most cookies bake at 400°F for about ten minutes, but that's because each one is only a couple inches wide, so the heat can easily be evenly distributed quickly, even at a high heat. When turning drop cookies into bar cookies, you need to lower the heat and cook for a longer period of time. Usually, 350°F for 30 minutes works well, but keep an eye on your cookies the first time you convert a recipe to make sure half an hour isn't too long. If the outer edges look over-cooked, but the middle looks undercooked, use 325°F next time.

Let the pan sit at room temperature for about 15 minutes to firm up after removing it from the oven. Then cut into squares in the pan. Set a timer for 15 minutes so you don't forget, because you won't be able to cut the squares neatly if the cookie pan has cooled completely. Making bar cookies takes about one-third the time that making drop cookies does because they are cooked in a single pan, rather than several, which means less time putting dough on pans, less time taking cookies in and out of the oven, and fewer pans to wash when you're done.

Bar cookies have the same taste and texture as drop cookies, but they are square.

Spread the cookie dough into a bar pan, leaving about an inch around the edges. Just as drop cookies get a little bigger during cooking, bar cookies also need a little room for expansion.

Use a sharp knife to cut the bar cookies into squares.

Snacks

If there is anything as challenging as desserts to pass up in the grocery store, it might be snack foods. It is fascinating that many grocery stores today have an entire aisle devoted to potato chips, candy, and other snacks, which have practically zero nutritional value and are loaded with fat, salt, and empty calories. Giving up potato chips was more challenging for me than giving up sweets, but it was easier once I realized that my craving for them was caused by hunger, which should be satisfied by something nutritious. I quit buying potato chips and other snack foods, although I do usually have some type of nut in the house, which serves as my emergency snack food. If I suddenly find myself starving and not wanting to wait until the next meal is cooked, I eat a couple of handfuls of nuts, which satisfies my hunger for an hour or two. Beyond that, the only snack foods we eat are those that we make ourselves.

I learned to make pretzels and crackers by accident. My son was making bread one day and told me that something was wrong with the dough because it wasn't rising. I took one look at it and said, "You didn't use any yeast." Oops! But in my typical "nothing is wasted" attitude, I asked myself what we might be able to make with a dough that has

Crackers

Makes about 3 dozen small crackers.

basic bread recipe excluding the yeast (page 86)
large grain kosher salt

Mix together all of the ingredients for the basic bread leaving out the yeast. Roll out the dough as thinly as possible in small batches and cut into squares, rectangles or whatever shape you want. Poke holes in the dough and sprinkle with large-grained kosher salt.

Bake at 400°F for 15 minutes. Remove the crackers that look done and return the rest to the oven for another 5 minutes. Because it can be a challenge to roll out the crackers uniformly, some of the crackers may be done before others.

no leavening. The family started brainstorming, and we came up with crackers and pretzels.

Soft Pretzels

Makes 8 to 10 large pretzels.

basic bread dough (page 86)
¼ cup baking soda

2 cups warm water
large-grain kosher salt

Make the basic bread dough with or without the yeast. I prefer the flavor without the yeast. If you use yeast, you can work with the dough immediately without waiting to let it rise. Oil your fingers and hands, and pull off a piece of dough about the size of a large egg. Roll it between your hands to create a long rope. In a small pot, combine the baking soda and water and bring to a boil. Dip the pretzel ropes one at a time into the baking soda solution. Place the rope on a cookie sheet that has been liberally oiled to avoid sticking. It can be placed as a long rope, or you can twist it into the traditional pretzel shape before baking. Sprinkle with large-grain kosher salt, and bake at 400°F for 10 to 12 minutes.

Caramel Corn

¾ cup brown sugar
¼ cup butter
¼ cup maple syrup or honey
½ teaspoon salt
¼ teaspoon baking soda

¼ teaspoon vanilla
8 cups popped corn

Melt the butter over low heat and stir to avoid burning it. Add the rest of the ingredients except for the popcorn, and stir to blend everything together. Pour the mix over the popcorn and toss to coat it well. Spread the coated popcorn onto a buttered cookie sheet and bake at 300°F for 15 to 20 minutes.

> **Savings:** Making your own snack foods will save you money in multiple ways. First of all, you will eat fewer snack foods because you probably won't make as many as you currently buy. And, of course, you will save money on the snack foods you make from scratch. Making a whole batch of organic soft pretzels will cost less than $1, which is less than a single soft pretzel purchased ready made.

Drinks

The healthiest, most ecothrifty choice for quenching your thirst is water straight from the tap in your kitchen or the water fountain at work. Unfortunately, consumers have been duped into believing that bottled water is safer or better than tap water. In reality, there are few regulations on the bottled water industry, whereas municipal tap water must be tested for quality and safety by independent laboratories, and the municipalities must release the results to the Environmental Protection Agency (EPA) and consumers.[29] Mistakes can happen in manufacturing processes, and there have been bottled water recalls that were instigated because of potential harm to human health. Bottled water has been found to be contaminated with a wide variety of pollutants from mold to bacteria and chemicals.[30]

Buying bottled water is definitely the opposite of ecothrifty because it costs one thousand to two thousand times as much as municipal tap water, and it takes a big toll on the environment because it is sold in plastic bottles that may leach chemicals into the water, such as BPA and di(2-ethylhexyl) phthalate, also known as DEHP[31] and end up in landfill sites. Unfortunately, only 13[32] to 20 percent of plastic water bottles are recycled.[33] If you have legitimate concerns about the quality of your tap water, you can buy a water filter to remove toxins. Although you can spend a lot of money on a filter, an inexpensive one will eliminate most toxins.

Soda

Most of us get bored pretty quickly drinking only water. A squirt of lemon or lime juice adds a nice flavor, but sometimes you want something more interesting. It is easy to conclude that soft drinks are the unhealthiest option available for the human body, as well as the planet. They are empty calories with artificial ingredients, and they use an enormous amount of energy in their production and transport. In addition to ingredients that are known carcinogens, many soft drink cans are lined with BPA and many of the plastic bottles are also made with BPA.

Americans consume an average of two and a half cans of soda at work every day,[34] and although cans are the most recycled packaging in the United States, only 58 percent of aluminum cans are recycled, which is better than the 31 percent of glass that is recycled, 29 percent of PET plastic bottles, and 6 percent of asceptic cartons.[35] If you like bubbly water, you have options. You can make soft drinks at home, saving money and the environment. You can make naturally fermented soft drinks using champagne yeast or the same yeast that you use for baking bread, or you can purchase CO_2 cartridges to force carbonation into water. Like commercial soft drinks, these will retain their effervescence if kept in a tightly closed container, so you can take them to work.

Home soda makers have grown in popularity over the past few years and are now available in many department stores, as well as online. They require no batteries or electricity and use bottles that are BPA free and can be reused for several years. You simply carbonate water if you want sparkling water, or you can add various flavors to the carbonated water to create cola, lemon-lime, root beer, and other popular soft drink flavors. Some of the less expensive syrups may contain artificial ingredients, but all-natural options are also available. The CO_2 cartridges are returned when empty, and they are refilled and resold, meaning zero landfill waste from them. Plain tap water makes up most of the soda, and one 500 ml container of syrup makes twelve liters of soda, saving fifty cans or six two-liter plastic bottles from the landfill or recycling center.

If you want more natural ingredients in your soda, add fruit juice to the carbonated water with or without additional sugar. For a stronger flavor, add concentrated fruit juice to the sparkling water. Concentrated soda syrup is also available through multiple sources online. Be sure to check the ingredients because some are naturally flavored and others include artificial flavors and colors; some have artificial sweeteners, while others have pure cane sugar or no sweetener at all.

Homemade soda can be put into a keg for large parties. Mix up the water, sugar, and soda flavor and pour it into the keg. Hook it up to the carbonation source and follow manufacturer's directions for dispensing.

You can also make soda using yeast to create natural carbonation. Although the finished soda does contain a very small amount of alcohol, it is less than one percent. When making homemade soda with yeast, put it in plastic bottles to ferment. If too much pressure builds up during fermentation, the bottle could burst, which could be dangerous if you are using glass. Natural fermentation takes a day or two to occur, so you have to plan ahead, but the process is quite simple. Combine ½ cup of sugar with a quart of water and ⅛ teaspoon of yeast in a repurposed plastic soft drink bottle. The sugar feeds on the yeast and ferments, which causes gas bubbles to form. You can add commercial flavors or natural lemon-lime juice, or crushed ginger for ginger ale.

> **Savings:** The sugar and yeast for a liter of soda costs only 16 cents, so based on the cost of whatever you use for flavoring, a batch of homemade soda can easily cost half as much or less than commercial soft drinks.

Coffee and tea

Tea and coffee are very popular drinks around the world, and they are frugal when made at home. Unlike soft drinks, they also have some health benefits when consumed in moderation. Many herb teas can be grown in your own backyard and air dried, eliminating any carbon footprint.

Despite the environmental costs of transporting black tea and coffee over long distances to North America, drinking tea and coffee is better for the environment than drinking soft drinks or bottled water because the amount of waste is minimal. The box or can in which the dry tea or coffee is purchased is small compared with the amount of tea or coffee that can be prepared from the dry tea leaves or coffee beans. Making tea or coffee at home and taking it along with you in a travel mug is the ecothrifty alternative to buying that take-out coffee in the morning. If you only want one cup of coffee at a time, coffeemakers that brew coffee in single servings are available.

> **Savings:** You can easily spend $2 to $4 on a cup of coffee or a cappuccino, whereas I spend $11 on 12 ounces of organic, fair trade, and shade-grown coffee. We use 0.9 ounces of coffee to make a 12-cup pot, which costs us about 80 cents for the whole pot.

Juice

In the past few years, more and more juice options have been showing up in stores. Obviously, "fruit drinks," which contain only artificial colors and flavors and no juice, are not nutritious or a good deal financially because they lack nutrition. However, over the past few years, newer juices tout nutritious ingredients. They may appear to be a good way to improve your diet inexpensively when the label says they contain a dozen different fruits and vegetables. Unfortunately, most of these are overpriced, especially when sold in single servings, when you check the amounts of the fruits and vegetables contained. One popular brand boasts 2600 milligrams of spirulina, 200 milligrams of broccoli, and another 200 milligrams of spinach in a thirty-two-ounce bottle, as well as hundreds of milligrams of other vegetables and herbs. Impressed? You shouldn't be. Two hundred milligrams is two-tenths of a gram, which is a piece of broccoli smaller than a peanut!

Blended fruit and vegetable juice is not the most frugal thing you can drink, but if you want to drink it, you should make it yourself because you can't buy vegetable juice that is as nutritious as what you can make at home with a juice extractor.

Savings: A glass of apple juice and a spirulina tablet will deliver about the same nutrients as a glass of a much more expensive green juice. A thirty-two-ounce bottle of the commercial green juice costs about $5 in my area, whereas apple juice can be purchased for about $1 per quart. Five hundred tablets of 500-milligram spirulina tablets are about $20 or about 4 cents per tablet, which would equal 20 cents for about the same amount of spirulina that is in the quart of commercial juice.

Beer

In the past decade home-brewing beer has caught on as a hobby for several reasons. Home brewers cite the quality of the beer they make themselves, the pride in making their own beer, and, finally, the money saved. The savings will depend on whether you make beer from extract or from grains, but the savings will be considerable. Home brewed beer can easily cost half as much as store-bought, but it would not be hard to save even more, depending on which method you use to make it. A kit with extract that will make about two cases of beer will cost $25 to $50, whereas the ingredients to make all-grain beer will cost $15 to $35, based on the type of beer you are making. A little more equipment is needed to get started with all-grain brewing, but it will last for years.

In addition, you are reusing bottles over and over again, and saving a lot of money and energy from being expended on shipping ready-to-drink beer from factory to store, much in the same way that drinking tap water is more ecothrifty than drinking bottled water. Because the main ingredient in beer is water, it makes sense to merely ship the other ingredients to a home where the water is already efficiently delivered via water lines.

Making beer from scratch is not as hard as it was a hundred years ago because today you can start out with kits that simplify the process considerably. Some people move on to brewing with grains, but others stick with the kits for many years.

If you're still nervous about trying it on your own, there are a variety of "u-brew" businesses where you can purchase ingredients and use their equipment to brew your beer. After two or three weeks, you return to bottle it. While the price per bottle might be a little more than if you make it at home, you don't have to invest in the equipment before deciding whether you will want to make more than one batch. You will also have an experienced person to guide you through every step of the process.

Tom Johnson of Maywood, Illinois, has been brewing his own beer for five years. "I used to ask a lot of questions about beer at restaurants and breweries. I didn't know how to describe what I liked and why," he explained. "A waiter at the restaurant told me that if I really wanted to isolate what is malty, hoppy, bitter, etc., I should brew my own batch of beer. So, I ordered a kit and will never forget sticking my nose into a bag of Fuggle hops; it got me hooked right away, even though that first batch turned out terrible.

"Brewing takes some creativity and patience as well as an effort to keep things sanitary. Learning how to brew all-grain was a challenge, but I think the results are like the difference between store-bought and home-baked bread. It is difficult to maintain a constant mash temperature until you get the rhythm of adding hot water (or can afford fancy equipment which I rebel against)," Tom said.

"Don't be afraid to fail. Keep at it and enjoy the process," advised Tom. "Listen to some good music that fits the style of beer or wine, for example, Bach with your Oktoberfest and the Chieftains with your Guinness clone. By all means have fun. It also doesn't hurt to brew with friends."

Savings: An all-grain beer-making kit for a dark amber beer sells for $28, and it makes about fifty twelve-ounce bottles of beer, which is about 56 cents per bottle. Compare that to your favorite German beer, which sells for more than $1 per bottle.

Wine

Even if you don't have your own vineyard, you can save money and resources by making your own wine. Once you have wine-making

If you decide to make your own beer, wine, or mead, you might think that you'll have to spend a lot of money on bottles for storing your fermented creations. But before buying any bottles, ask your friends to give you their empties. As soon as we started our first batch of wine, we mentioned to friends that we'd be happy to take their empty wine bottles, and by the time our wine was ready for bottling, we had enough donated bottles that we didn't have to purchase any. And friends continued giving us their empty bottles for months, so we didn't have to buy any for subsequent batches. You could also ask at your favorite restaurant.

equipment, which will cost around a hundred dollars, you can make wine for less than a dollar a bottle if you have your own grapes or fruit. However, you can still save a lot of money by using wine-making kits, concentrated juice, or even fresh fruit that you purchase. Bottles from store-bought wine can be reused to bottle your wine, but you will have to buy new corks for every bottle.

Making wine with a kit is a great way to start because it eliminates one very big job — crushing the grapes or other fruit to extract the juice. This also eliminates the need to purchase a crusher, destemmer, and press, which cost several hundred dollars. Of course, you can crush fruit the old fashioned way just like Lucy in the famous episode of the 1950s sit-com, but it is rather messy and imprecise, and then you have to strain it through a cheesecloth or old pillowcase. Using a juicer is a bad idea because odds are good that you will kill the machine by the time you're done. You really need at least a gallon of juice for making wine, and if you have ever used a juice extractor, you know it is rather slow. It is easy to see that having the right equipment would make the process much easier.

In addition to starting with concentrated juice, the kits are nice because they come with instructions and all of the additional ingredients that you need, such as bits of oak so you don't have to buy an oak barrel for achieving that oaky taste. We made our first wine with a kit, and I'm glad we did because it simplified the whole process. And if you don't want to make wine at home, there are u-brew businesses for making wine, where you will be assisted and provided with all the equipment you need from fermentation to bottling.

Cheryl K. Smith of Low Pass, Oregon, has been making fruit wines for about fourteen years, using mostly blackberries, rhubarb, apples, and elderberry, which grow on her property, but she has also used peaches that she purchased or strawberries that her parents have grown. "I also have had really good luck with what I call 'clean out the freezer' wine," Cheryl explained. "You use up last year's frozen berries."

Denise Schrader of southwest Missouri has been making wine for about three years and usually uses concentrated fruit juice like her grandfather did. "I always make at least twelve gallons per batch and make two to three batches a year of assorted kinds. I did however make the best peach with real fruit," Denise explains.

Ellen Malloy of Chicago began making fruit wines about four years ago after learning to make beer and soda. She also makes wine with flowers, such as dandelion and elderflower. She says the best thing about making her own wine is, "the sense of independence I have with what goes into my body and also the connection I have with the American past. Things like strawberry wine were made in the Midwest for all time before the seventies, when wine started taking hold in America. It is fulfilling to connect with that."

"I recommend that anyone who wants to try it just jump right in," Cheryl says. "It is hard to ruin wine, unless you are not careful with sterilizing your tools and carboys."

"Be patient," advises Denise. "The wine will let you know when it's ready for the next step. Don't rush it or it could be ruined. It is really a quite easy process, and there is nothing better than opening a bottle and knowing that you made it yourself."

Savings: Wine-making kits produce wine at a cost of $1.50 to $5.00 for a 750-ml bottle, saving about 80 percent on a bottle of wine.

Mead

Mead, sometimes called honey wine, was probably the first fermented beverage made. The main difference between mead and beer or wine is that mead uses honey to feed the yeast. Making mead uses equipment and principles similar to making beer or wine. If you've already invested in the equipment to make beer or wine, you probably have what you need to make mead. As with beer and wine, you can buy kits to simplify the process.

Beyond food

Having the right tools makes any job easier and more fun, and cooking is no exception. I make my own mayonnaise, but I honestly can't imagine doing it without a blender, although I know it can be done with a whisk.

C. Milton Dixon of Chicago has been making mead for about eight years. He prefers making mead to making beer or wine because he can use locally foraged ingredients, such as crabapple, serviceberry, lemongrass, chokecherry, garden huckleberry, wild grape, elderberry, motherwort, mugwort, creeping charlie, and one he calls "X-marks-the-spot," which includes mugwort, motherwort, caraway, juniper, and hot pepper.

Like most people who make fermented beverages, Milton said it was not hard to learn. "Fermentation is a natural process that has been harnessed for thousands of years. It will happen in spite of everything you do. Usually worst case is you get vinegar instead of alcohol."

It might be a good idea, however, to start a batch when you know you'll be home to keep an eye on the fermentation process. "There was the time that I made a batch of wild grape mead, then set off to visit some family for Thanksgiving. We had someone house-sitting our cats, who don't get along at all. At some point the airlock got plugged up and exploded, shooting dark purple ferment all over the ceiling and then frothing over onto the floor. When our house sitter came the next day, they opened the door to see dark pools of liquid on the floor and thought the cats had killed each other. We had quite a mess to clean up when we got home."

I push a button and in about a minute, I have mayo, compared to whisking for who knows how long. In addition to the things I have listed here, think about what else you might need to make it easier and more enjoyable to prepare your own food.

Cookware

It didn't take me a terribly long time to decide that there were problems with inexpensive non-stick cookware. The non-stick surface wears off within a few years, and you are left with pots and pans to which food will stick. I was left wondering where those tiny bits of non-stick surface went.

My favorite cookware is made of cast iron or stone. A couple of my cast iron skillets were picked up at garage sales or estate auctions, while some were passed down from my parents, and I bought others. Cast iron cookware will last practically forever — it is not an exaggeration to say that it can last a hundred years or longer. It can also be used on top of the stove or in the oven. A cast iron Dutch oven lets you brown meat for a casserole on top of the stove and pop it into the oven for the final baking. A cast iron skillet can be used on the stove, and it can also be used as a pan for baking a cake or cornbread in the oven.

One of the things I love about cast iron is that it is naturally non-stick, but you have to know how to use it. Patience is key because you need to cook over low to medium heat. New cast iron was probably pre-seasoned, but if the label does not indicate that, or if you bought it used, you should put a thin coating of oil on it before using it. It is also a good idea to put a very thin coating of oil on it regularly after washing and drying.

Never put cast iron in a dishwasher or let it air dry because it will get a small amount of rust on it. Although this won't harm it long term, you'll have to wash it again before you use it, which is a waste of time. Because a tiny bit of black will rub off when you dry it, you can either have a towel dedicated to your cast iron cookware or use a paper towel that you toss into your compost. The black residue is not harmful when cooking, and studies have shown that additional iron winds up in your food, especially acidic foods, when you cook in cast iron. After washing my cast iron pans, I set them on one of the burners of my gas stove so that the bottom is definitely dry before I put it away.

Almost all of my baking pans are stoneware. Most are unglazed because like cast iron, stoneware is porous, which means it can become seasoned and naturally non-stick. The only caveat about the non-stick part is that if you have absolutely zero fat in a recipe, such as the French bread in this book, you will need to spread a thin layer of cooking oil on the stone before baking, or you will have a bit of a challenge with the baked bread sticking to the pan.

Glass is another environmentally friendly option for baking, but food will stick to it if you don't oil it. Food also seems to cook a little faster in glass, so be sure to check for doneness about five minutes before the recipe suggests doing so.

> **Savings:** Although you can easily spend more than $100 for a high end non-stick skillet, I recently saw one at a discount store for $29. A new cast iron skillet at the same discount store costs only $16. Before discovering the beauty of cast iron, I'd buy the less expensive non-stick skillets every two or three years, replacing them as the non-stick surfaces wore off — and it wasn't just a single skillet. I had entire sets of non-stick cookware, which wound up costing me more than $100 every few years to replace.

Ovens

If it feels like you overcook (or undercook) everything, you might need an oven thermometer. Ovens are usually quite accurate when brand new. However, within a couple of years, a variety of things may start happening with your oven that will make it less than accurate. You will know when the thermostat is not working perfectly if you have an oven thermometer. They only cost a few dollars, and they can save you a lot of heartache caused by meals that don't meet your expectations. If the oven consistently heats to a temperature that is different from where you set the thermostat, you will know to compensate by setting the thermostat higher or lower in the future.

It's common that over time the seal on the door starts to wear out, and heat escapes. You wind up with undercooked food in the front of the oven and overcooked food in the back. A new seal is not very expensive, and you can easily replace it yourself. Having a good seal on the oven door also saves money by saving energy.

Dishes

The better you feel about eating at home, the more you will eat at home. One way to make it more appealing is to have pretty dishes, which make dinner look nice. You can prepare delicious meals at home and easily present them as elegantly as a meal in a five-star restaurant. There is no reason to wait until Thanksgiving to use fine china. If you don't pull it out of the cabinet at least once a month, it will get so dusty in there that you will have to wash it before you use it next time. It hardly seems fair to have to wash dishes twice for a single meal, so we use china for dinner at least every three or four weeks. And complete sets of dishes for every day use can be found often at garage sales or estate auctions for an incredibly good price.

Napkins

My husband and I have been using cloth napkins for as long as I can remember. One of the things I noticed as a little girl was that nice restaurants had cloth napkins, and fast food restaurants had paper napkins. I always wanted to emulate the nice restaurants, so of course I loved the idea of cloth napkins. But they are also an ecothrifty choice. Many of my napkins came from garage sales, and the rest were bought on clearance. Although they do have to be washed, they have hardly any ecological footprint because being so small, they can be added to any wash load without affecting the amount of detergent, water, or energy needed. And because they don't usually get very "dirty," they don't need to be washed after every meal. In most cases, each person can continue to use the same napkin for the entire day.

CHAPTER 6

Home

Most of us spend the majority of our time in our homes, and we spend a huge amount of money on appliances, maintenance, cleaning, electricity, and other utilities. We can save a lot of money by making more ecothrifty choices in this part of the household budget.

Air fresheners

Not only are air fresheners a waste of money, most of them also contain a lot of multisyllabic chemical ingredients that are not healthy for you. Many fragrant candles also contain toxic chemicals. If your house is clean, it does not stink. You need to find the cause of odor and eliminate it, rather than try to cover it up.

More than a decade ago when we moved to a new Chicago suburb, we decided to rent out our old house rather than sell it. It seemed like a good financial decision at the time, but the renters trashed the place. When they moved out, the stench was horrible. The house was so badly messed up that it required some remodeling, and when we pulled out the kitchen cabinets, we discovered one of the main sources of the odor — dead mice and mouse excrement. Once the mice and the excrement were removed and the area was cleaned, the house again had a normal smell.

Pet urine is one of the worst odors to deal with and one of the reasons we don't have carpet. If a dog or cat repeatedly pees on a section of carpet, it may need to be replaced. In the meantime, baking soda sprinkled on it will absorb some of the odor.

When my oldest child was a toddler, I purchased a child's wooden table and chairs for her at a garage sale. It appeared to be in perfect condition sitting in the sunny driveway, but when I took it home and put it in her bedroom, the room quickly smelled of cigarette smoke. I diluted vinegar with 50 percent water, spritzed every surface with it, and wiped it down, eliminating the odor.

> **Savings:** If you currently buy air fresheners, you will save whatever you've been spending on them by simply eliminating them from your purchases.

House plants

Because many modern homes are so well insulated, indoor air quality can actually be toxic. However, it's been known for about thirty years that houseplants are natural air cleaners. In addition to turning carbon dioxide into oxygen, plants can also absorb pollutants like ammonia, benzene, formaldehyde, toluene, trichloroethylene, and xylene. Because different plants absorb different chemicals, it's a good idea to have a variety, including peace lily, snake plant, cornstalk dracaena, English ivy, spider plant, and elephant ear philodendron. Tropical plants work especially well because they are accustomed to the low light environment that exists in most homes. Research by NASA recommended fifteen to eighteen plants in the average home.

Appliances

It may seem that the ecothrifty way of doing things would be to use electrical appliances as little as possible, and that is true up to a point. In some cases, however, using energy efficient appliances can help you save money and use fewer resources.

Increasing energy efficiency

Buying energy efficient appliances is made easier by the Energy Star rating system, a program jointly run by the US Environmental Protection Agency and the US Department of Energy. The Energy Star tag on an appliance states how much energy the specific model uses, allowing an easy comparison of products for selecting the most energy efficient model meeting your needs.

All appliances, whether rated energy efficient or not, will save energy if you turn them off when you are not using them. Appliances that have a remote control or a clock are never off when plugged in, so you save money by unplugging them when not in use. While small appliances, like a coffeemaker or a microwave oven, may use only two or three watts per hour, many appliances in stand-by mode use as much electricity as a small light bulb.[36]

Although these numbers can vary somewhat from one model to another, here are a few examples of how much energy is used per hour by appliances:

	Stand-by	On
Television	10 watts	100 watts
DVD player	7 watts	12 watts
Modem	14 watts	14 watts
Computer & peripherals	15 watts	130 watts
Laptop	2 watts	29 watts[37]

There are several strategies that will reduce the energy consumption of an electric hot water heater.

@ **Reduce the temperature** — This will save money on your electric bill and will also reduce the risk of scalding yourself or a small child.

@ **Use a timer** — This can be used to turn off the water heater during the hours you are not likely to be using hot water. For example, if you usually are sleeping from 10 p.m. until 6 a.m., you can set the timer so that the heater turns off from 10 p.m. until 5:30 a.m. Because water heaters are well insulated, there will be hot water available when the heater is turned off, but water in the tank won't be reheated until the timer turns the heater back on.

◉ **Add insulation** — Most modern water heaters are well insulated. However, if you have an older one, or if you can feel any warmth on the outside of the water heater, adding a jacket on the outside increases the insulation and will save more energy by reducing heat loss.

Dishwashers

Although studies have been done by various entities from governmental agencies to nonprofits concluding that modern Energy Star rated dishwashers save energy, water, and money over hand washing, many individuals remain skeptical. The skeptics have two main arguments. The first is that they use less water when washing dishes by hand. I don't doubt that this is possible, but I don't think most people try hard enough to actually accomplish that. Do you know how much water it takes to fill up your sink? One side of mine will hold seven gallons with room to spare. True, I do have a rather large sink, but if you want to wash dishes by hand, you need a large sink to hold your skillets and baking pans. A gallon of water in my sink is one inch deep, which is barely deep enough to immerse a dinner plate. Modern dishwashers only use about four gallons per cycle, which is hard to beat. Hand washing dishes can use 5,000 gallons of water more per year than using a dishwasher.[38]

The second complaint that people have about dishwashers is that it takes a lot of resources and energy to manufacture an appliance that winds up in a landfill at the end of its useful life. Unfortunately, there is no argument to counter this complaint. It's a frustrating fact. But it is offset by the benefits of water conservation delivered during the dishwasher's lifetime, combined with energy saved not having to heat the additional water used by hand washing.

Even though modern dishwashers save energy compared to their predecessors, they can save even more energy if users follow a few simple guidelines. All manufacturers now say that rinsing is not required before putting the dishes into the machine. Even though you only need to scrape food from the plate, most people report still rinsing dishes before putting them in the dishwasher. Even if the dishes are going to sit in the dishwasher for a while before being washed, the "rinse" cycle on the dishwasher uses less water than rinsing the dishes individually in the sink and prevents food from drying on dishes. Using the air dry function rather than the heated dry option will also use less energy.

Freezers

Purchasing an energy efficient freezer can pay for itself by allowing you to store garden produce and buy foods in bulk. Although the chest freezer was the obvious choice for energy efficiency not too many years ago, uprights have become more energy efficient, so compare Energy Star ratings on the models you are considering for purchase. Chest freezers tend to be less expensive than an upright for a similar amount of storage space, probably because most people find the upright easier to organize and more convenient to use. You have to bend over to get things out of a chest freezer, and it can be difficult to find something when it is almost full.

Someone once asked me in an interview if using a freezer is really a green practice because freezers use electricity. Most of us live in a climate where we either need to preserve our locally grown food for eating during the winter or to buy food that has been transported thousands of miles. An Energy Star rated twenty-cubic foot freezer will only use 434 kilowatts and cost $46 annually to operate, based on 10.65 cents per kilowatt hour.[39] The freezer is definitely the ecothrifty choice if you are using it to store locally produced food.

Cleaning

We all want our homes to be clean, and there are plenty of commercial products available to help us meet that goal. However, most of them are filled with dangerous chemicals that can cause allergic reactions, skin irritation, respiratory distress, and other health problems. And they pollute the environment. There are many natural alternatives available. Entire books have been devoted to the topic, providing the reader with dozens of recipes for homemade cleaners. However, making your own cleaners doesn't need to be complicated, and you don't need to mix up a different type of cleaner for every surface in your house. Vinegar and baking soda will take care of most of your cleaning needs. Borax and washing soda will take care of the rest.

Actually, a wet cloth and a little muscle take care of more cleaning tasks than you might expect. Several years ago, my husband asked why we spray cleaner on a mirror before wiping it, and when I didn't have an answer for him, he decided just to wipe it clean with a wet cloth and dry it with a towel. It worked and the mirror was shiny. For things that are not truly dirty, such as a countertop that has a bit of flour on it, wiping clean with a dishcloth can work just as well as using a commercial cleaner.

Cleaning things regularly helps to avoid build-up of dirt and grime. Using a toilet brush in the bowl of the toilet on a daily basis will keep the toilet clean without using any cleanser. If the bowl has stains that are not coming out by scrubbing with the toilet brush, add a quarter cup of borax and let it sit for fifteen minutes before scrubbing again. When I suggested daily cleaning without a commercial product to a friend, he asked, "what about germs?" Although the makers of commercial toilet

---

A word about sponges — don't! Not only are sponges unnecessary in a kitchen, they are a perfect home for germs. Sponges start to stink because bacteria are growing on them. It is possible that your countertop may wind up with more germs on it after wiping with a sponge than it had beforehand. Using antibacterial dish detergent may kill bacteria in your sponge, but it is not necessarily good for your skin when washing because it kills the good bacteria along with the bad, and many experts recommend against using antibacterial cleaners. Dishcloths can also pick up bacteria but can be laundered after a day's use and are a safer alternative for washing dishes and wiping down countertops in the kitchen.

bowl cleaners would like you to believe a commercial product is necessary for a sanitary bathroom, the simple fact is that the bowl is "sanitized" only until the next time the toilet is used.

Vinegar and baking soda can do the majority of cleaning in a home. Vinegar is an acid, and baking soda is abrasive, so between the two of them, most cleaning needs are taken care of.

- **Countertops** — To clean and disinfect a countertop spray it with diluted vinegar and wipe clean with a dishcloth. Why does vinegar disinfect? Because it's an acid, and most germs don't thrive in an acid environment.
- **Coffeemakers** — To clean an automatic coffeemaker and keep it running smoothly, fill the water reservoir with one part vinegar and two parts water. Put the carafe in place and turn on the coffeemaker. After the vinegar-water solution has run through the machine, fill the reservoir with water to rinse out the vinegar. Some sources suggest doing the rinse twice, but usually I need to do it only once to remove the vinegar residue.
- **Dishwashers** — To clean dishes in a dishwasher make a detergent mix of equal parts of borax and washing soda and store it in an airtight container. (See page 125 for more on using borax and washing soda.) To use, fill up the detergent cups in the machine and run the dishwasher as usual. Although this has worked well for me, some people use only a tablespoon of the mix in each dispenser cup, saying that using more leaves a white film on the glasses. This detergent mix works especially well in hard water and keeps the inside of your machine free from mineral deposits. Using vinegar in the rinse-aid dispenser will prevent hard water spots on glasses and will protect the dishwasher from hard water build-up during the rinse cycle. And although the savings on dishwasher detergent aren't huge, many commercial brands contain chemicals, such as chlorine bleach, that I don't want on my dishes.
- **Sinks** — To clean the kitchen sink and drains, fill a teakettle or small pot with water and heat to boiling on the stove. Sprinkle baking soda

on the bottom of your sink and into the drain. Use a dishcloth or pad to scrub the sides and bottom of the sink. Pour a cup of vinegar over the baking soda and into the drain. It will start to foam and may even bubble up out of the drain like a little volcano. When the foaming stops, pour boiling water into the sink, rinsing the bottom and flushing the drain. Not only does this clean and disinfect the sink, it also keeps the drain running smoothly so that it doesn't get clogged or start stinking from fat and food particles that get stuck in the trap at the bottom of the drainpipe.

◉ **Stovetops** — To clean the stovetop, sprinkle a small amount of baking soda on it and scrub with a wet dishcloth. Clean areas of cooked on food by spraying with vinegar and letting sit for five minutes before wiping clean. Stubborn cooked on food might need to be removed with a plastic scraper after spraying and letting sit for a longer period of time.

> **Savings:** Commercial dishwasher detergent costs 9 to 24 cents per ounce, whereas homemade detergent is 6 cents per ounce.
>
> A brand name glass cleaner is 19 cents per ounce, and a brand name all purpose cleaner is 12 cents per ounce, whereas water is free, and vinegar costs about 3 cents per ounce, so the commercial window cleaner costs more than ten times as much as a fifty-fifty vinegar/water mix.
>
> Brand name powdered scrubbing cleaners cost 10 to 45 cents per ounce, whereas baking soda costs about 6 cents per ounce.

Laundry

Laundry is needlessly expensive for two reasons — the cost of detergent and the cost of running an electrical dryer, both of which are also hard on the environment. But there are alternatives to commercial laundry detergent and electric dryers, and there are other ways you can save money while making greener choices about doing your laundry.

Detergent

Searching for homemade laundry detergent recipes online could keep you busy reading all day. Making your own laundry detergent is becoming quite popular, and when you talk to people who do it, they say two things. First, it saves a lot of money, and second, it is incredibly easy to do.

Most recipes are made with three basic ingredients: washing soda, borax, and soap. Washing soda is sodium carbonate, which is very similar to sodium bicarbonate, more commonly known as baking soda. A lot of people say you can use either one. Washing soda is available in many grocery stores and discount stores in the aisle with commercial laundry detergent. It has been around since the 1800s and is sold today as a laundry detergent booster.

Borax is another cleaner that has been around for a very long time. I used to presoak cloth diapers in it when my children were babies, and the diapers stayed white and fresh smelling for all the years I used them on three baby bottoms.

Many recipes include a bar of soap that you've grated. I don't add the soap to my detergent mix, however, because I don't want to take the time to grate a bar of soap, and I find the detergent works well without the addition of the soap.

I didn't think the soap was really necessary because today most people do not get genuinely dirty. Yes, we sweat, but most of us don't get dirt and grass and blood stains on our clothes daily. Seeing great results

Laundry Detergent

Use ⅛ cup for a regular load of laundry.

2 cups washing soda
2 cups borax

Put the washing soda and borax into an airtight container and shake to blend.

in my clothes and even in kitchen towels that had been stained with food, I decided to test the homemade detergent even more. We live on a farm, so I've used this detergent to wash clothes that are stinky and dirty, stained with all sorts of bodily fluids after attending goat births, and the clothes come out clean.

This blend does not create suds, so don't worry when you don't see any. However, you might see suds the first time you use it because it is washing out the detergent residue in your clothing. The washing soda/borax blend can be used for delicates, baby clothes, and in hard water. In fact, both borax and washing soda are natural water softeners.

Pretreat a very dirty item before throwing it into the washing machine by wetting it and rubbing it with bar soap until sudsy. If you have an entire load of laundry that is really dirty, add one-quarter cup of borax to the load or do a prewash with one-quarter cup of borax. Presoak single items in a gallon of water with a tablespoon of borax. Blood usually rinses out of stained items easily after soaking in cold water. For more challenging blood stains, hydrogen peroxide does the trick.

Of course there will be some stains that won't wash out, even if you use the most toxic chemicals on the market. This is why we need to relearn the old-fashioned concept of having play clothes, work clothes, and nice clothes for dressing up. You don't need spotless clothes for working in your garden or cleaning house.

> **Savings:** Commercial laundry detergents cost 24 to 41 cents per load, depending on the brand. Using one-eighth cup of a fifty-fifty blend of washing soda and borax costs 13 cents a load, decreasing your laundry detergent costs by 50 percent or more.

Softeners

Fabric softeners are a great example of corporate advertisers creating a need for a product. Why do your fabrics need to be softened? I remember seeing the television ads as a child and believing that static cling was a horrible problem. When we started using cloth diapers on our first baby, we learned that we should not use fabric softeners because it would decrease the absorbency. Logically, we then decided we shouldn't use it on towels either. Eventually we stopped using fabric softeners entirely at our house, and we never noticed a difference in the clothes other than the disappearance of the strong perfume smell that most fabric softeners impart. In the middle of winter when the air is especially dry, polyester clothing will sometimes cling to other fabrics, but once you pull the items apart, the problem is usually solved. Once or twice in the past ten years I've had a skirt that was clinging to my legs, but I didn't feel it warranted purchasing chemical laden fabric softeners on a regular basis. I simply changed clothes.

For those who find they do need a fabric softener, white vinegar can be used. Add up to one-half cup to the rinse cycle. Some people put a ball of wool or a ball of clean, used aluminum foil in the dryer to eliminate static cling.

> **Savings:** Dryer sheets cost 4 to 7 cents each, and liquid fabric softeners cost 13 to 17 cents per load. If you do five loads of laundry per week, that adds up to 260 loads per year for a savings of $10 to $44 per year.

Temperature

It might seem obvious that washing in cold water saves energy, but did you know that about 90 percent of the energy used for washing clothes is used for heating water? A front-loading, Energy Star rated washing machine actually uses very little electricity. If you are skeptical about cold water getting your clothes clean, start with a few loads that don't appear particularly dirty.

> **Savings:** You can save $80 to $100 per year by using cold water to wash your laundry.[40]

Drying

Drying clothes can cost a small fortune if you use a power-guzzling electric or gas dryer. However, clothes can also be dried for free. I can't think of too many practices that have been more maligned and associated with a lower class lifestyle than hanging clothes on the clothesline. In fact, some communities prohibit clotheslines. And this is unfortunate. I refer to my clothesline as my solar clothes dryer. People have a number of complaints about clotheslines, but these are usually due to lack of information.

- **Clothes and towels are too stiff and scratchy.** — If this really bothers you, toss them into the dryer on "air" for about ten minutes after they're dry. The "air" setting uses very little electricity, and the tumbling action will soften the fabric. But when you think about it, you might not want your towels to be that soft. At a spa you'd have to pay to get the kind of exfoliation on your back or feet that you can get free using a clothesline-dried towel. I love my loofah-like towels and actually miss them during the winter when our towels are dried in the dryer.
- **Clothes take too long to dry.** — Actually, they can dry just as fast on a clothesline on a sunny day as in your dryer. If it's sunny and windy, they can dry even faster than in a dryer!
- **It takes too much time to hang up and take down clothes.** — Hanging up clothes does take a bit of time. However, most people lead lives that are far too sedentary already, so a little exercise is a good thing. As for taking them down from the line, if you fold them as you are taking them down, you are handling them only once, and it does not take any longer to do than it would to pull them out of the dryer and fold them.
- **A clothesline is not practical year-round where I live.** — Take advantage of the free solar energy when it is available. We use our clothesline seven or eight months a year, which means we save two-thirds of what we previously spent when we used our electric dryer year-round. You could also consider a dryer rack or clothesline in your laundry room or basement for winter air-drying.

⊚ **Some clothes will be wrinkled if dried on a clothesline.** — These are clothes that probably look best ironed, even when dried in a dryer. Iron these clothes straight from the washing machine after spinning. It doesn't take any longer to iron them wet than it does to dry them and then iron them, and they look really crisp afterwards, even without using starch.

There is no need to buy an expensive umbrella-style spinning clothesline. The old-fashioned style with two T-posts and four lines works well. Be sure to site it above a clean grassy area so that if an item falls off the line, it won't get dirty. And if you happen to have a neighbor who grills outdoors frequently, you might want to take that into consideration so that you don't wind up with smoky clothes.

> **Savings:** Line drying your clothes, saves 30 to 40 cents per load over an electric dryer, or 15 to 20 cents per load over a gas dryer.[41]

Light bulbs

Nine years ago we decided to change all of the incandescent bulbs in our house to compact fluorescent light bulbs, sometimes called CFLs, and we saw an immediate decrease in our electricity bill. Compact fluorescent bulbs use less than one-fourth as much electricity as their incandescent cousins. For example, a thirteen-watt fluorescent bulb puts out 825 lumens of light, which is comparable to a sixty-watt incandescent bulb that emits 840 lumens. At a rate of 10 cents per kilowatt hour for electricity, you will save $37 in electricity over the life of the fluorescent light bulb, which is estimated to be about 8,000 hours. CFLs also produce 90 percent less heat than incandescents,[42] which I find especially important during summer months.

When compact fluorescent bulbs were first introduced, consumers had several objections, such as price, which has decreased dramatically in recent years, although the initial cost per bulb is still four to five times as much as an incandescent. The early bulbs also did not turn on instantly. The one- or two-second delay was enough to stop some people from using the bulbs. Instant-on bulbs are now available, although some still require a few seconds to reach full brightness.

People also complained that like all fluorescent bulbs, the compact bulbs contained a small amount of mercury, which created a disposal hazard. Although CFLs do contain mercury, it is one percent of the amount that is in an old-fashioned mercury thermometer.

As recycling programs grow across the United States and Canada, proper disposal of CFLs is easier than ever. Some retailers are even starting to accept used CFLs. A quick online search should yield some positive results for disposal sites in your area. Because CFLs last so much longer than incandescent bulbs, disposal is not a frequent activity.

Compact fluorescent light bulbs are an obvious green choice, but they are not the only choice. LED light bulbs are available for home use. LEDs use even less electricity than CFLs. However, we have not been able to find many locations in our home to use them because the light output of these bulbs tends to be dim. We have two, three-watt bulbs in our living room. They stay on most of the evening providing adequate light for walking through the area but not enough light for reading, conversing, or any other activity. LEDs are popular as landscaping lights that can be powered by small solar cells.

I remember one of my high school teachers would leave the lights on in our classroom when we went to the library. When I asked why he didn't turn off the lights to save energy, he said that it would take more energy to turn them back on than to leave them on for the hour that we were gone. Unfortunately, a lot of people still believe this myth today. The fact is that you should turn off lights — fluorescent or incandescent — if you will be gone from a room for more than a few minutes. These lights do draw a bit more current when being turned on, but this amount pales in comparison to the amount of energy used if lights are left on for extended periods of time. A light that is left on all the time will need to be replaced sooner than if it is turned on only when you are in the room. In the end, you will save money on your electric bill and in bulb replacement costs by turning off the lights when you are not in the room.[43]

Savings: Although CFLs cost more than an incandescent to purchase, they will last ten times longer than an incandescent, and they use one-fourth as much electricity.[44]

Heating and cooling

Most of us have spent our entire lives simply moving a dial on a thermostat to control the temperature of our homes, but there is more we can do to avoid using energy for heating or cooling. When we built our house, we situated it on an east–west axis so that we would get solar heat gain during the day from the sun shining into the south-facing windows. On a sunny day during the winter months, the passive solar energy causes the temperature in the house to increase by two degrees above the temperature that the thermostat is set at. During the summer, the sun is high in the sky for most of the day and two-foot eaves keep it from shining into most of the windows.

Natural heating and cooling

Changing the axis orientation of a house is not an option unless you are doing new construction. But there are other ecothrifty options for heating and cooling your home.

- **Fans** — An attic fan works well in climates where night temperatures are at least ten degrees cooler than daytime temperatures. Open the windows and turn on the attic fan to pull cool air into the house at night.

  Ceiling fans make a room feel several degrees cooler than what the thermostat reads by moving the air around, and even small tabletop fans can make a room feel cooler.

- **Windows** — Even if you don't have an attic fan, you can open and close windows to control the temperature in your house. Open windows when the temperature goes down at night and close them in the morning when the temperature is forecasted to go above 80° F during the day to trap the cool air inside.

◉ **Window coverings** — A variety of window coverings can also be used to control temperature. We have insulated blinds, which we close on the east side of the house in the morning so that the rising sun doesn't heat up the interior. Late in the afternoon we close the blinds on the west side of the house. Having insulated blinds or draperies can also help insulate your house from the cold in the middle of winter. Closing them at night when temperatures fall and there is no sun shining into the windows reduces heat loss.

Cooking strategically

Before the invention of central air conditioning, many homes, especially those on farms, had a summer kitchen, which was apart from the main house and was used in the summer to avoid heating up the house during cooking. Although most people in modern society do not have the inclination to build an old-fashioned summer kitchen in their backyard, they do have the ability to cook outside. Outdoor grilling is popular, and I love it because the house stays cooler and less humid when we avoid cooking in the kitchen.

On hot summer days, our family cooks as many meals outside as we can dream up, preparing all sorts of meat and vegetables on the grill. A couple of years ago when we replaced our old grill, we bought one with a side burner so we can also boil or sauté foods outside. And I recently bought a cast iron pizza pan so we can use our grill to make pizza during the summer. The pan can also be used as a griddle, so we'll be able to make flat bread or tortillas outside also. We can even make pancakes on the griddle or eggs in a skillet on the side burner for breakfast.

You probably won't save any money if your grill is hooked up to a portable propane tank because the cost per gallon is considerably more than what you pay for natural gas, which is available in cities, or propane, which people use to heat their homes in the country. Our grill is hooked up to our house propane system, so the fuel cost is the same whether we cook a meal on the stove or on the grill. If you already use natural gas for heating or cooking, you can run a line to your deck or patio and hook it up to a grill. When you purchase the grill, check to be sure that it works with natural gas. If you already own a propane grill, you can buy a conversion kit from the manufacturer so that it will work with natural gas.

> **Savings:** It can be tough to calculate the savings from cooking outside, but our house stays much cooler through the summer if we don't cook indoors during the day. If you have air conditioning, you will save on the extra time it will have to run if you are cooking indoors and heating up the house.

Thermostats

For the same price as an old-fashioned manual thermostat, you can get a programmable thermostat that allows you to change the temperature setting for various times of the day. Of course, you can get fancy if you want to spend more money. You can buy thermostats that have a touch screen, are Wi-Fi ready, and can be controlled via the Internet from a computer anywhere in the world. The less expensive models will work fine for most people, though. The programmable thermostat can be set to a lower temperature when you are at work or sleeping so that you are not wasting energy to heat an empty house or a home where everyone is in bed under warm blankets.

A thermostat on each floor allows different temperatures to be set throughout the home. A floor with only bedrooms can be kept at a lower temperature except for the short periods of time when people are going to bed or getting up, so you can save a lot of money by reducing the thermostat setting in winter during the day and the middle of the night.

Furniture

Twenty-seven years ago, I bought a new table and four chairs for my first apartment for $199. The set was very sturdy. Today with the proliferation of discount stores, you can still buy a table and four chairs for that price, but it is far from being a sturdy set. Furniture that is cheap in terms of both price and quality is plentiful. It falls apart within a couple of years, goes to the landfill, and is replaced by more cheap furniture. The answer to this problem has as much to do with attitude as with strategy.

Instead of filling up your home with cheap furniture that won't last, you can buy used furniture from yard sales, thrift stores, and auctions. Other than spotting a listing for free furniture, yard sales usually provide the best deals. People are sometimes so anxious to get rid of old furniture that they almost give it away. Several years ago I bought a lovely upholstered chair at a yard sale for only $5. Learning to reupholster furniture is on my to-do list, but in the meantime, the chair sits in my bedroom and gives me a place to sit down when changing clothes. It is very sturdy and in excellent condition, but is upholstered with outdated fabric.

Well-cared-for antiques often provide excellent value. Unlike new furniture, which depreciates from the moment you take it home, antiques maintain their value or increase in value as they age. After moving to the country I discovered the excitement and joy of auctions.

Refinishing Furniture

Teresa M. Smith of Adams, Minnesota, has been refinishing furniture since she was sixteen years old. "My mother was refinishing furniture for people, and she asked if I'd like to help out and she'd pay me 50 cents an hour. The money attracted me and I found I enjoyed doing it. . . . I did countless pieces of furniture before I was married. Once married, I refinished my own furniture as I started my family." In addition to refinishing furniture, Teresa has also done kitchen cabinets and windows.

If you are just learning to refinish furniture, it is probably easier to start with furniture that was originally stained, rather than painted. Teresa said it is much harder to remove paint if there is not a coat of varnish underneath it. Depending on the hardness of the wood and size of the wood grain, paint can be almost impossible to remove.

Estate auctions are common in rural areas, probably because it is the easiest way to liquidate not just a household but also farm equipment and sometimes even livestock and the land itself. Some communities also have auction houses that regularly host auctions. You should be able to find auctioneers in your area and keep an eye on the schedules for upcoming sales. Generally, a list of items to be auctioned is available in advance so that you can get an idea of whether it would be worth your time to attend. It's a good idea to arrive early to look over the items and be sure they are in good condition and that you will be able to use them for whatever you need. A piece of furniture that is too large to fit through your front door isn't such a great deal after all!

Antique dealers often attend estate auctions to buy furniture for resale in a shop. At the first estate auction I attended, I saw a beautiful marble-top dresser similar to ones selling for a thousand dollars or more that I'd admired in antique stores. At the end of the day, I was the ecstatic owner of that dresser, as well as a few other antiques that I never even dreamed I could afford. In some cases, only one person was bidding against me — usually an antique dealer. The wonderful thing about auctions is that generally everything will be sold that day, regardless of the price, so you can get some incredibly good deals. The downside is that you might come home with something you really didn't need — like a pump organ — because it just seemed like too good a deal to pass up.

With the recent resurgence of bedbugs, you should probably avoid buying used mattresses and definitely do not pick up a mattress that was put into a dumpster or set out with the garbage. It may be in the trash because it is infested. It is always a good idea to carefully look over any article of furniture you are going to buy — new or used — with a bright light to be sure you don't see any bugs. They can also hide in cracks of wood furniture. Buying new furniture, however, is not always a guarantee of avoiding bedbugs. One scenario for getting bedbugs from new furniture is the department store delivery truck that takes away old mattresses when delivering new ones. If a used mattress is infested when it is put in the truck to be hauled away, the bedbugs can infest the truck and crawl onto the new mattresses being delivered.

Savings: You can save hundreds of dollars by purchasing furniture at auctions, second-hand stores, and yard sales.

CHAPTER 7

Gardening

There are few things you can do in this world that offer as much reward, financially and personally, as gardening. A tomato seed, which costs only pennies, can grow into a plant that can produce twenty or more pounds of fresh, organic food. In addition to the financial benefits, gardening provides you with a reason to go outside, breathe fresh air, and get some exercise. And once you've tasted a garden fresh tomato, you will understand why it is the number one vegetable grown in backyard gardens. But the benefits don't stop with tomatoes. Practically every vegetable tastes better when it's fresh and ripens on the vine, and it is more nutritious. From the time produce is picked, it starts to lose nutrition, and if it is picked green, it has lower nutritional value than if it is vine ripened.

Sometimes articles or books make gardening sound like a terribly expensive hobby, requiring high-priced tools, raised beds, and gravel-lined pathways. In reality, you can start growing some of your own foods for less than $10 by purchasing a few inexpensive bedding plants at your local garden center. If you have never had a garden, start small with your favorite, most-often purchased vegetable. Nothing is more disappointing than seeing a garden consumed by weeds because it was too big for you to be able to tend through the growing season.

Savings: How much money you save will depend on what vegetables you grow. If you plant easy-to-grow, prolific, and expensive vegetables like bell peppers, you will save a lot more than if you plant inexpensive vegetables like carrots, which yield one carrot per seed and can be a challenge to germinate. Assuming half a pound of fresh produce per square foot of garden space, you can expect about 300 pounds of produce from the average 600-square-foot garden. At $2 per pound, that adds up to $600 of fresh produce. The average investment for a food garden is $70, providing you with a savings of about $530 annually.[45]

Small spaces

You may think that you need a big yard to have a garden, but you can grow vegetables in almost any space that you have, provided it gets sun. Even if you have no yard at all, you can grow plants in pots on a balcony or in front of a sunny window.

A backyard vegetable garden does not need to be large to produce an abundant harvest. The key is in planning the garden design. You can plant more in a small space by creating wide rows or by growing vertically.

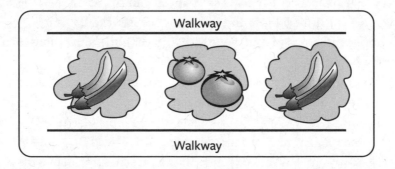

Plants that are very bushy and produce lots of little fruits, such as tomatoes and bush beans, generally work best planted in a single row because it makes harvest easier when you have direct access to all sides of the plant.

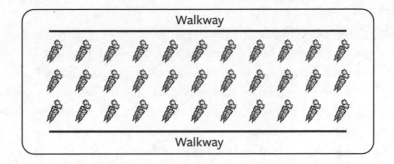

In the traditional garden design, plants are lined up in a single row with a wide aisle between the rows, which means the majority of the space in your garden is used for walking rather than for growing. In wide row gardening, the dynamics are reversed and the majority of space is used for growing plants. Root crops work especially well in wide row gardening because they can be spaced fairly close together, and because the plants are not bushy, it is easy to harvest them.

Salsa Garden

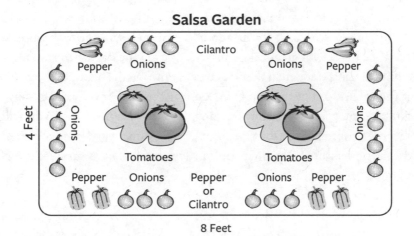

This diagram for a salsa garden illustrates how planting in wide rows permits more plants in a smaller space. You might be able to get a third tomato plant in this space, but by putting only two tomato plants here, there is plenty of room to put pepper plants (either hot or sweet), onions, and herbs in the open areas. This design works best with determinate tomatoes, which don't get as big as indeterminate tomatoes.

Vertical gardening

Just as the name implies, vertical gardening means growing plants upwards on trellises, arbors, fences, teepees, and whatever you can imagine. Although pole beans may immediately come to mind when you think of climbing vegetables, cucumbers and vining winter squash are also good candidates. Even though I have plenty of space in my garden, I like growing cucumbers on old fencing panels because they are easier to harvest when they are not growing all over the ground. If you grow especially large winter squash vertically, they may need a little extra support as they grow. Old nylon hosiery can be used to make a sling to cradle the squash and attach it to whatever the squash is climbing so that gravity doesn't pull the squash from the vine before it's ready.

Cold frames and low tunnels

It is possible to harvest vegetables year-round, even if you live in colder climates, such as Michigan or Maine, by using a cold frame or low tunnel, both of which are unheated by anything other than the sun. A cold frame is a box with a glass top, and a low tunnel is a short hoop house that is covered with greenhouse plastic. During the day when the sun is shining, heat is trapped in the structure, so during the night, the warmth of the ground keeps the plants inside from freezing even though temperatures may fall well below freezing. By adding a row cover, you will trap even more heat in the soil, which will protect your plants to even lower temperatures. The plants in our low tunnels have survived overnight temperatures as low as −15°F.

Container gardening

Even if you don't have a yard, you have a variety of options available to you for growing at least some of your own food.

Try container gardening. If you have a south-facing porch, deck, or window, you can create a beautiful and delicious pot of vegetables, strawberries, or herbs. There are even varieties of some vegetables that are made specifically for pots, such as "patio tomatoes." If you don't have a place to sit a pot, you can use hanging planters. Pots come in all sizes and shapes.

I have one that is long and narrow and made specifically for growing on a windowsill. You don't even have to buy a pot. You can repurpose a bucket or other container by drilling a few holes in the bottom for drainage. I've seen all sorts of things used as pots, including coffee cans, milk cartons, and frozen orange juice containers. You will need to use a good organic potting soil and fertilizer and remember to water frequently.

Containers planted with edibles can be just as attractive as those planted with non-edible plants. Okra planted in a pot will grow five feet tall and produce blossoms that look a lot like Rose of Sharon.

Greens Pot

Even a pot as small as 12 inches across can be productive. Divide the surface into thirds, and plant seeds in each section. For a colorful display, put several Swiss chard seeds in one third; plant red romaine lettuce in another third; and plant kale in the last section. When the plants are a couple inches tall, add more seeds between them so that you can have a second harvest after cutting the first plants.

Sprouts

A lack of outdoor space is not a barrier to growing some food. You can grow sprouts in a jar in your kitchen for a fraction of the cost of buying them in the store. Sprouting seeds are sold at health food stores and through online vendors. To grow alfalfa sprouts, put two tablespoons of seeds in a quart jar, add a couple of ounces of water, and close the jar with a sprouting lid or tie a piece cheesecloth over the opening. After soaking overnight or for ten to twelve hours, pour off the water. Two or three times a day rinse the sprouts. You don't want to leave them standing in water between rinsing, but you also don't want them to dry out completely. Sprouts that haven't been rinsed for a couple of days will probably need to be tossed into the compost. The seeds sitting in water in the bottom of the jar will have started to rot, and if they have started to sprout, the seeds on top will have dried out completely and died. I leave my sprouting jar on the kitchen counter next to the sink so I am unlikely to forget about it.

Edible landscapes

Why spend time and money feeding and watering a lawn only to spend more money cutting it every week when you could replace it with fruits and vegetables? Before you skip to the next section, swearing that you will never have rows of corn in your front yard, let me say that I am not suggesting anything of the sort. I immediately thought of the Garden of Eden the first time I saw a yard that fully employed the concept of permaculture. Eggplant, tomatoes, and onions grew under a young plum tree. A variety of herbs and salad greens grew along the side of a pond. Vegetables and herbs were interplanted with each other, and anyone driving past would have assumed this was a traditional flower garden. Get creative and think beyond rows and rectangles when planning an edible landscape.

Community gardens

Many years ago when we first moved to the Chicago suburbs, we lived in an apartment and rented a plot at the local community garden so that we could grow at least a few vegetables. Community gardens are available in many communities, usually at a very reasonable price. In fact, the plots tend to be very popular, so there is a waiting list in some cities. It can be a challenge to remember to tend a rented plot because it is not conveniently located just out the door. This can be overcome, however,

Yard Sharing

We co-coordinate a summer leadership training for young adults called Summer of Solutions, which is part of a larger program called Grand Aspirations and runs in different formats in nineteen locations across the US. In the summer of 2011, we got the idea to develop a land-sharing model where neighbors in our community could offer their land for others to grow food on in exchange for some of the food themselves. We piloted the program with one yard this past summer and converted roughly 700 square feet of urban lawn into a cornucopia of fresh, organic vegetables. The food helped feed our   ☞

summer staff while providing an excess for us to share at public events we held in a demonstration garden down the street from our growing site.

Throughout the process, we developed a small set of tools for working with landowners. One of the most important of these has been a template for a land use agreement between the owner and the gardener. We also created liability release forms for any person the gardener brings on the property. Some of these documents are overkill, but in an age of civil lawsuits, we wanted to make sure we could allay the concerns of every potential landowner we may come into contact with.

This next year, we plan to expand our program, bringing in up to ten more landowners and connecting them with families who have a desire to grow but do not have access to land. Our methodology will be to canvass blocks of single-family homes and adjacent multiunit apartment buildings to find people willing to make this connection. Our program team will also be developing the skills and resources to assist with the garden build from start to finish.

This solution is something that really grows organically out of the structural nature of our community. Rogers Park, where we live, is a mixed-income neighborhood with a wide variety in housing stock. We offer a free garden education program for low-income children in the area and would really like to develop the land-sharing as a means for connecting their families with an opportunity to engage in growing their own food. Since many of the kids live near blocks with single-family homes, we hope to plan this year's growth around their particular areas.

— Peter Hoy and Molly Costello, Chicago, Illinois

if the plot is located in an area that is between your home and place you travel to frequently, such as work, school, or the grocery store.

Saving seeds

Although seeds are not very expensive, you can make your garden even more economical by saving seeds from one year to the next if you grow heirloom varieties rather than hybrids. The easiest seeds to save are those from plants that are self-pollinated. You can easily save seeds from beans, peas, eggplant, greens, lettuce, peppers, and tomatoes. Some plants, such as mustard greens, will even reseed themselves year after year. So although they are annuals, you plant them once, and they renew themselves every year. Squash plants cross-pollinate easily, so if you had more than one type of squash plant in your garden, seeds saved from them will not necessarily reproduce the parent plant.

Keep in mind that genetically modified (GM) plants are patented, which means you are prohibited from saving their seeds. You will know if you buy GM seeds because you are required to sign an affidavit swearing that you will not save the seeds or give them to anyone else. This inability to harvest seeds for the next season is reason enough to avoid purchasing them, let alone the health concerns related to GM plants.

Composting

You can provide your plants with all the nourishment they need by using compost, also known as black gold, instead of expensive and possibly harmful chemical fertilizers. There are two basic things you need to know to create compost: first, stuff rots, and second, the bigger the pile, the faster it rots. I know there is a lot of information written about carbon-to-nitrogen ratios and things like that, but if you pile up any organic matter (stuff that used to be alive) three feet high and three feet wide, it will rot. Even if you have the perfect carbon-to-nitrogen ratio, the pile will take years to rot if it is not big enough. A pile that is at least three feet in all directions will heat up to 130°F to 150°F on the inside, and the plant matter in the middle of the pile will decompose rapidly, killing harmful bacteria and weed seeds in the process. Compost will be ready to use in a few weeks if the pile is turned or fluffed up regularly, making sure the material on the outside winds up on the inside.

> **Savings:** Compost is free, whereas enough fish emulsion to cover 300 square feet costs about $11.50 at my local garden center. Compost will also help you save whatever amount you previously spent on mulch because it can do double duty.

Lawns

The lawn has been a part of the European landscape since the 1700s, and North Americans were quick to emulate them. Initially it was only the very wealthy who could afford the maintenance required for a lawn because it was all done by hand, but with the invention of machinery and chemicals in the twentieth century, a pristine lawn became the norm for virtually everyone with a yard. However, it comes with a high price ecologically and financially, as well as time spent on maintenance and the risks associated with the chemicals used.

Deciding not to maintain a lawn is simply not possible for many people because of homeowner association rules, municipal codes, and the wrath of neighbors. So, what can an ecothrifty person do? Avoiding chemicals is the easiest way to save money because there are usually no rules or ordinances mandating their use. You will only have to deal with the raised eyebrows of neighbors when the dandelions are blooming in the yard.

An old-fashioned reel mower is the most ecothrifty option for maintaining a lawn. We used a reel mower when we lived in the suburbs. It works well on city- and suburban-sized lots, and there is not the deafening drone of a power mower. The caveat, however, is that you must mow the lawn regularly because a reel mower cannot handle the grass if it gets too tall. This may mean cutting it more often than once a week during seasons when it is growing especially fast.

If your lawn is too large for a reel mower, an electric mower is a more environmentally friendly option than one powered by gasoline. Although an electric mower initially costs more to purchase, it costs less to operate because the cost of electricity is far less than the cost of gasoline, and this difference will continue to increase as the cost of gas is increasing faster than the cost of electricity.

If you have a riding lawn mower, you probably know that it is a gas hog. And it is the worst when it comes to creating air pollution from emissions. When we first moved to the country, we bought a riding mower and mowed about two acres every week. It didn't take long for us to realize how bad it was for our budget and the environment. Most of our yard is now garden or pasture.

Lawns can be converted to attractive and productive garden space. Instead of converting the lawn to an edible landscape by planting fruits and vegetables, another option is to replace grass with plants native to your area, such as succulents and cacti in the desert Southwest or prairie plants in the Midwest to create a hardy and low maintenance garden.

Savings: Our electric mower costs only 3 cents to charge, meaning we pay less than a dollar a year to mow our lawn, which is now less than half an acre. By canceling the service of a company that sprays chemicals on your lawn, you can save several hundred dollars a year. If you are able to eliminate your lawn and replace it with native plants, you will be able to save everything you previously spent on fertilizer, herbicides, mowing, and other maintenance. And if you replace it with an edible landscape, you will save even more in food costs.

CHAPTER 8

Entertainment

Prior to the invention of the radio and television, people made their own entertainment and once in awhile they would attend a play or a dance. Only the extremely rich spent a great deal of time pursuing leisure activities, such as riding horses for fun or playing cards. But even they created most of their own entertainment by having dinner parties, talking to friends, and playing musical instruments. Today we want to be entertained, so we listen to music, watch television, and attend movies, concerts, and plays.

When people ask me how I have time to do all the things I do — garden, raise animals for meat, dairy, and eggs, as well as write and speak regularly — the first thing I generally say is that I don't watch television. That may sound like a simplistic answer, but it is entirely true. There was a time when I watched six to twelve hours of TV every day, and I accomplished little in my life. I spent my childhood watching television. I'd come home from school and immediately flip on the TV to watch reruns of the popular 1960s and '70s sitcoms until the news came on, which was when I'd do my homework and eat dinner. Then in the evening, I'd watch television until I went to bed. On the weekends, I'd watch from ten or eleven in the morning until ten in the evening or later. And we only had three channels when I was growing up. When I had small children, I kept the television on for much of the day.

When my oldest child was six years old, she was well on the road to growing up watching as much television as I did, but one day everything changed. I learned that she had written a "love letter" to the little boy across the street because she'd seen a girl do it in a TV sitcom. That's when I realized that my children were learning a lot more than I wanted them to learn by watching whatever happened to be on the tube at any given hour. We canceled our cable subscription and never looked back. We kept our television in the family room, and we used it to watch videos at predetermined times. Rather than living our lives around the television schedule, we began actually planning our viewing.

The problem with having a hundred or more channels from which to choose at any given hour is that whenever you turn on the TV, there is bound to be something showing that you would like to watch. The average American watches more than 150 hours of television every month.[46] That adds up to almost three, forty-hour workweeks. What could people do with even half of those hours if they were not watching television? Do the math for yourself, though. Write down the times you have watched television over the past week and add up the hours. Become a conscious consumer of television. Ask yourself which shows you really want to watch.

Television can be a positive part of our lives if used thoughtfully, and watching TV can be an ecothrifty form of entertainment. Consider downloading movies or renting them, rather than buying DVDs, which will eventually wind up in a landfill along with the packaging. And how many times do you really plan to watch the same movie? Some libraries have videos available to borrow or to rent at a cheaper rate than for-profit companies.

> **Savings:** In addition to saving electricity by not watching so much TV, you will have more time to do things that are productive, and research shows that you will actually reduce your spending on discretionary purchases and junk food.

Hobbies

Research has found that people who engage in hobbies and active leisure activities are happier than those who engage in passive leisure activities, such as watching television. If you have a hobby (or two or three), you are probably not surprised by this finding. Hobbies, such as playing musical instruments, quilting, sewing, spinning, knitting, crocheting, weaving, woodworking, rebuilding a car, gardening, and cooking, give us a feeling of accomplishment. Some people might look at this list and wonder why gardening or cooking is mentioned — that's work, not a hobby! But it is all a matter of perspective.

Looking back at my teen years when I taught myself to cook from the recipes I found in Better Homes and Gardens, I realize there was a very big difference in the way that my mother and I viewed cooking. When I looked at photographs of artistically arranged food in magazines, I wanted to duplicate it, much the same as wanting to make a scarf or quilt after seeing a picture of it. My mother viewed cooking simply as a chore. The more I learned to cook, the more excited I became about learning more. Not only did I enjoy the compliments I received, but I also enjoyed being able to eat meals at home that were more delicious than what I could get in almost any restaurant. But it was slow going. I didn't start cooking regularly until after my first child was born and I began to learn about the benefits of eating a more nutritious diet. Not every meal at our house is an artistic production, but I still think of cooking as fun, rather than a chore to be avoided.

At this point in our lives, not only do my husband and I enjoy cooking food from scratch, but we also have fun making our own cheese and wine and growing our own fruits and vegetables. Although it is usually true that you love what you do well and you do well what you love, gardening was a huge challenge for me. I kept trying in spite of one failure after another because I wanted all the beautiful and delicious heirloom vegetables that were unavailable in stores.

When I lived in the suburbs, I took our dogs to obedience classes. Today, I spend my time taking care of goats and chickens and other animals, which provide us with eggs, meat, and milk for food. Although caring for animals is my idea of fun, there are other hobbies that can help you save money and reduce your impact on the planet. In modern society we no longer have to make our own clothes, grow, fish or hunt our food or even cook for ourselves. Activities that used to be chores now fall into the category of hobbies, and they happen to be activities that support an ecothrifty lifestyle.

Quilting has long been a popular hobby. Although many quilters today buy fabric specifically for making a quilt, historically quilts were made from scraps, either new fabric that was left over from another project or fabric from old clothes. In addition to being ecothrifty, you can create a special keepsake and family heirloom when you make a quilt from scraps. A quilt is also a practical gift that can be used every day,

Cynthia Simpson of Pleasant Plains, Illinois, made quilts for each of her children as they graduated from high school. Although she made one from new fabric, the rest were made from a variety of scraps, such as pieces of fabric left over from other projects. She also bought ties at a secondhand store to make a quilt for her youngest daughter.

Using T-shirts she saved from throughout her son's childhood, Cynthia made this quilt for her youngest son. "It was a sentimental history of his childhood," Cynthia says.

Savings: Making a quilt from old shirts will cost you only the price of batting and fabric to cover the back of the quilt and possibly space between quilt blocks, depending on the pattern you use. Batting for a full-size quilt can be found online for less than $10, and the backing fabric will be around $20 or $30. If you were to buy a hand-made quilt of the same size, it would cost several hundred dollars, but it would have no emotional value for the recipient.

reminding the user of the special meaning behind the fabric. Making quilts from children's clothes works especially well because children tend to outgrow their clothes long before they are worn out, meaning that the fabric still has many years of life.

Leftover fabric, old clothing, and used sheets can also be turned into rag rugs, keeping them out of the landfill and creating something useful for your home. A quick Internet search will turn up several different ways to make rugs from fabric strips. Whether you want to braid, crochet, sew, or some combination of the above, there is a method that you can learn.

Hobbies can wind up turning into a business venture. I started making soap for myself, and I gave a few bars to friends as gifts. Almost immediately people started asking if they could buy my soap. Several of my friends have had the same experience and now earn money sewing clothes, felting, and quilting.

Music

More than a century ago if you wanted to hear music you either had to attend an event where music was played or you had to make your own music. Many people played instruments for their own entertainment, from the harmonica to the piano. When we lived in the suburbs, my daughters took lessons in playing the violin, piano, and flute, and my oldest would pick up and play any instrument that happened to cross our threshold, from the cello to the fife and recorder. The sound that emanates from a portable media player or even a CD player pales in comparison to the glorious sounds of live music in your home. Never assume that you are too old to learn to play a musical instrument or that you have forgotten too much of what you learned when you took music lessons at an earlier age.

If you enjoy listening to music, consider downloading it on your computer or portable media player. Although one CD may seem like a small thing to send to the landfill, think about how much music can be downloaded. Imagine all of the hundreds of CDs that can be replaced by downloading music, and then think about the landfill space used for disposal, the energy and resources needed for manufacturing, the pollution created by manufacturing, and the fossil fuels burned in the distribution of CDs.

Rita Hoover of St. Charles, Illinois, gets together with four friends every week or two to make music together. "It's such a feeling of accomplishment when we play a piece well, but it is also just a whole lot of fun to work together for the fun of it — we laugh often and encourage each other," Rita says. "Wine is usually involved, as well. I'd highly recommend dusting off that old instrument you haven't touched in years."

Kelley McClure, who splits her time between Texas, and Alicante, Spain, feels similarly. "There is such a freedom and release from stress when playing your instruments in your own private time. I like to play the sax in the evenings by the fireplace, with a nice glass of red wine," she explains. "On the other extreme, I also like playing the clarinet in an orchestra with the stress of rehearsals and ultimate performance."

Savings: Although the price of a CD is very similar to the price of downloading an album, you can save money with downloading because you can download only the songs that you want.

Books

Sharing resources is the ecothrifty way, and libraries are based on this principle. In addition to books, today's libraries offer a full range of media — music, movies, ebooks, access to computers, ereaders for loan — and offer a range of programming, from storytime for preschoolers to educational lectures. And most libraries are on bus routes, making it eco-thrifty to get to them.

Our family loves books. We have been buying books for our children since before the first one was born. Although we initially bought them only at bookstores, we quickly learned about library book sales. Used books are typically quite inexpensive, and we attended one that sold books for $5 a bag or $15 per box for the last hour of the last day of the sale. We brought home a lot of books that day! You can sell books online or to secondhand bookstores when you decide you no longer need them.

Some homeschooling groups have a book sale or book swap every spring. There is no reason you couldn't organize a similar event for children in your neighborhood or the public or private school that your child attends. Like the clothing swap (page 50) you set the rules and let everyone know how it works in advance. Will you be selling books that are donated and giving the money to a charity or children's group? Or will you swap an equivalent number of books for each child that donates books? For example, if you bring five books, you can take home five books.

Ebooks save a lot of trees because one ereader can now hold the equivalent of hundreds of books, and if you use an ereader that can transfer books to and from your computer, you can have thousands of books without any paper being used. Ebooks usually cost less than "real" books. If you don't want to buy an ereader, you can download books to your computer after downloading free software from sites that sell ebooks. Other books are available online as PDFs. Thousands of titles are available free of charge. Most of them are classics that are no longer under copyright, but sometimes publishers offer newer ebooks free for a very limited time to get word-of-mouth publicity from readers.

> **Savings:** Most ebooks currently cost a little more than half as much as a "real" book, but this field is constantly evolving and changing. Although you do have to factor in the cost of the ereader, this price has been falling fast and may continue to fall until it is a moot point.

Computers

Although new technology is not perfectly green because computers contain some dangerous metals and usually travel halfway around the world to reach the consumer, they do provide us with many opportunities to reduce the rest of the stuff in our lives. A computer today can take the place of a stereo, thousands of DVDs and CDs, a television, a telephone, several bookcases, thousands of books, a few filing cabinets, and hundreds of reams of paper, ultimately saving dozens of trees and keeping a lot of trash out of landfills. Think about this before you purchase your next computer. Can you avoid buying a television if you upgrade to a larger computer screen? Or could you avoid buying a new stereo if you upgrade the speakers on your computer?

> **Savings:** If you are able to use a computer to replace and consolidate the functions of a television, DVD player, stereo, bookcases, and filing cabinets, you can save hundreds of dollars.

Celebrations

We all have special occasions to celebrate throughout the year, and it can be tempting to overspend. Instead of feeling that you're depriving a loved one of something by not purchasing a lot of disposable products, think about how classy your soiree can be by using table linens and attractive dinnerware. For an especially large get-together, start cooking days or weeks ahead of time so that on the big day you can pull out a delicious home-cooked feast that will have everyone wondering how you did it.

Birthdays

I can't think of any other event that can derail a usually ecothrifty parent the way that a child's birthday party can. Parents who may not ordinarily purchase any disposable paper products beyond toilet paper can find themselves buying paper plates, cups, napkins, tablecloths, streamers, and decorations, along with plastic eating utensils and goody bags filled with more plastic, or candy made with artificial ingredients. Why do they do this? Because they think that the children will be upset if they are faced with food and a party atmosphere to which they are unaccustomed. Most parents who do manage to buck this trend, however, find that children have just as much fun without all of the usual birthday party trappings.

Instead of using a commercial character for a theme, use something generic, such as fairies, pirates, or cowboys. Cathy Lafrenz, owner of a pick-your-own flower farm in Donahue, Iowa, held a Victorian tea party for a little girl and her friends. The guests all dressed up for the occasion, and during the party they decorated straw hats with silk flowers to match their outfits. They also made flower vases by decorating jars with supplies left over from previous craft projects or purchased at a secondhand store.

"So the mason jars were decorated with ribbon and paint and beads and buttons," explains Cathy. "They threw art supplies on a table and let the kids go wild! It was so much fun to watch. Then the girls cut flowers for their vases as the glue dried and took home inexpensive vases full of flowers."

Party decorations were the usual vintage linens and dishes used for all of the adult tea parties at the farm. "All of our table linens, dishes, stemware and silverware come from donation, resale shops and thrift stores."

"Instead of goody bags you can fill a themed item — a purse, a pot, a bucket or pail," says Kelsi Nibbana of Columbia, Maryland. "Also, making a craft is good to do instead of goody bags. We potted plants at one of my daughter's parties. Last year we had an insane sleepover with eight girls and they each got a book." You could have each of the children decorate a T-shirt with fabric markers, or you could give each one a puzzle to take home.

For a couple of different birthday parties, we served make-your-own pizzas for the children. We made crusts ahead of time and chopped up a variety of toppings and shredded cheese, and during the party, each child made his or her own pizza. The children loved this because they were able to put exactly what they wanted on their pizzas. Making your own ice cream to go with a homemade cake is fun because many children have never seen ice cream made from scratch, so it is entertaining for them, as well as practical.

> **Savings:** The more you opt out of the commercial birthday scene, the more you can save. You could easily spend $50 on paper products, another $50 to $100 for a commercial bakery cake, and even more on goody bags. You save all of that by not using disposable party supplies or buying a cake!

Holidays

For parties at our house, whether for adults or children, I have thirty inexpensive plates that I purchased more than twenty years ago. They are stored in the basement when not in use. Rather than buying plastic ware, I have extra flatware, and I have tablecloths that were purchased either on clearance or at yard sales. In addition to keeping hundreds of paper plates and plastic forks out of the garbage over the last two decades, I've saved $20–30 for every party we've hosted. And whenever we are planning a get-together, I know I don't need to buy those things.

Productive hobbies provide a ready supply of gifts for birthdays and holidays. For Christmas one year my daughter knitted beautiful tea cozies, one for me and one for her aunt, and she knitted scarves for her cousins. Handmade gifts usually cost less than those bought in a store, and they can become treasured family heirlooms, such as handmade baby blankets and quilts. You could create a number of different gift baskets filled with homemade preserves or other home canned foods, as well as cookies or fresh bread. Similarly, you could fill a gift basket with

Tea cozies insulate a pot of tea and keep it warm. This tea cozy was knitted by my daughter, but patterns are also available for crocheting or quilting a cozy for the tea lover in your life.

Food tends to be a huge part of any holiday celebration, so much so that you may be tempted to purchase quite a bit of prepared food. But there are alternatives. One year when we were planning a large holiday celebration, my youngest daughter and I started baking cookies two months ahead of time. Each week, we would double a cookie recipe and freeze half of the cookies. We had the immediate reward of having cookies, and we had a full batch of cookies in the freezer waiting for the holiday party. By the time the party rolled around, we had seven different types of cookies to serve!

homemade bath and body products. The time you put into your hobby, whether it is baking bread, making soap, or canning jam, will reward you with ecothrifty gifts.

Picnics

When you need a change of pace, how about having a picnic rather than going to a fast food restaurant? Every summer our family attends the Illinois Shakespeare Festival, and one of my favorite things is to have a picnic on the lawn of Ewing Manor before the play, which is held in an amphitheater. We take Portobello mushroom and chevre cheese sandwiches or mozzarella, tomato, and basil on crusty French bread, as well as pasta or rice salad, and cookies or brownies for dessert. We pack it all in a cooler with a bottle of wine and glasses. I pack glass or china plates into the cooler by placing a cloth napkin between each one, which protects them from breakage and makes it easy to hand out plates and napkins during the picnic. For vacations when our children were small, we would take road trips with a cooler full of food and eat our lunches on the picnic tables at rest areas along our route.

Savings: Like any home-cooked meal, you'll save money by preparing a picnic rather than eating out. The picnics that we have before the Shakespeare plays during the summer wind up costing us less than $10 total (minus the wine), whereas it would cost the four of us more than $50 if we ate out at a restaurant. And the same bottle of wine served in a restaurant would cost about four times as much!

CHAPTER 9

Transportation

We have more choices than ever before when it comes to traveling from point A to point B. The most ecothrifty choice is to walk or ride a bicycle when traveling short distances, and mass transit works well for longer distance travel. However, if you're like most people in modern society and have had a car in your life forever, living without one may seem inconceivable.

Alice Hollowed, of Chicago, decided to get rid of her car in 1998 when she found herself paying $250 a month for parking. She described her car-free experience:

> I started taking the bus to work and made friends with my morning bus driver. He would actually wait for me if I ran late. When I met my husband, he didn't have a car either. When we got married and bought a condo, we made sure to buy something close to the "L" so we could stay car free. When we had a baby, we figured we would buy a car when we needed one. We figured the longer we did without one, the better, especially since we were going down to one inner city public school teacher income. Four kids later we still don't have a car. These days we really enjoy the lifestyle of not having a car. We can't do as much stuff, so we don't.

We don't play chauffeur or run a million errands. We find that we save a lot of money. We live very comfortably with just one income. The environment has also become very important to us.

Alice said it took her a while to figure out how to use public transit effectively, and it can be tricky with children. Having a stroller on a bus is particularly challenging, but she discovered babywearing, and that has made a positive difference. She has a variety of baby carriers, which she uses based on the baby's age. She also has different strollers for different uses, such as an umbrella stroller for trips that will involve a bus, and a double stroller for when they will have a lot to carry. Like many cities, Chicago has a car-share company that rents cars by the hour, and Alice's family has used it occasionally. She also shops online, which she feels saves them money because it is easier to compare prices online than when shopping in stores. They thought that having their fourth baby might be their undoing, but they survived, so they don't see buying a car anytime soon.

Todd Allen of Chicago, Illinois, decided to stop driving in 2003. Going car free was surprisingly easy for him:

I bought a bicycle trailer for hauling groceries and other local shopping. I started using public transit when the weather was really foul. My socializing changed somewhat from far-flung suburban friends and activities to more local friends and activities. I had increasingly found time spent driving to be aggravating and all of the costs and hassles of maintaining a drivable car annoying. It was wonderful to eliminate it. I've since built a large bicycle trailer capable of hauling anything that I could carry in my car. I pull the trailer with a tricycle with an electric assist system. Bicycles and mass transit fully meet my transport needs.

Chicago video artist Lynn Stransky decided to go car-free in college. "It was simply impractical for me to own a vehicle since almost all my needs could be met on or very near to campus, and parking was a nightmare," Lynn said. "When I graduated and moved into Chicago, my roommate and I had the choice to get a car, but after much discussion, we decided against it."

Although it can be challenging not to own a car sometimes, like when they're building a set for one of their projects, Lynn and her artist collaborator have figured out how to make it work. "We built these structures mostly from two-by-fours, two-by-sixes, and plywood, which was, of course, not on hand," she explained. "We had to bring the lumber from the store to our house a little over a mile away. When no one with a car was available to help, we had some of the wood cut to more manageable dimensions, loaded it up in a cart, and simply pushed the cart to our house. I think it's important to note that we are both very petite women — I'm five feet; she's five feet, four inches — and weigh less than 225 pounds combined, but we were still up to the task."

Jerry, a college student from Chicago, started using a scooter when he was a teenager. He found that the cost of gas for the scooter turned out to be about the same as riding a bus and gave him more flexibility. The only thing he didn't like about it was that due to its small engine size, it was not allowed on highways, so he always had to stick to side streets. When he went to college, he decided to use a bicycle. He figured that the

Do you need a car?

Fill in the blanks with actual or estimated costs and compare the total to see if it would save you money to go car-less. If you are thinking of buying a car, you can get prices from car dealers, payment information from lenders, and an insurance estimate from insurance companies based on your driving record and the make and model of car.

Monthly car payment	____	Monthly mass transit for commute	
Monthly insurance payment	____	to work	____
Monthly gasoline	____	Monthly taxi fare for special trips	____
Monthly prorated annual maintenance costs	____	Monthly car rental for special trips	____
Total	____	Total	____

money he would have spent on insurance and gasoline could be used to buy a new bicycle and that he could use the exercise. In addition to that, his father wanted the scooter to use himself!

Car sharing

Car shares, which may be businesses, cooperatives, or non-profits, are popping up in cities and on university campuses in North America, Australia, and Europe. It is a less expensive alternative to renting a car from a traditional car rental company. In most cases, you become a member by paying an annual fee, and then you pay an hourly or daily rate, which usually includes gasoline and insurance. There are no rental offices, and cars, trucks, and vans are typically located all over the city or campus, making it convenient to find one nearby. You reserve a car online or by phone, finding a car near you to reserve, and your personal membership card or key fob will unlock the car. In addition to being used by people who have chosen not to own a car, a car share membership can be an ecothrifty alternative to a second car in families that don't use their second car often.

Carpooling

Whether you have a car or not, carpooling may be an option for you if you can connect with someone who lives in your area and works near your place of employment. There are websites online that match up people, and some large corporations may even have carpool matching available. If you are nervous about sharing a ride with a complete stranger, ask for references and check them out on Facebook or LinkedIn. You should also meet in person in a public place to discuss compatibility and logistics. Who will drive and how often? Is it okay to eat, drink, or smoke during the drive? What about the radio? With a little planning you could cut your commuting costs by 50 percent or more, and with carpool lanes on many highways, you might even have a quicker commute.

Ecothrifty driving

Location is obviously very important if you are going to live without a car. If you live in the suburbs, a small town, or in the country, mass transit may not be available and walking or biking may be impractical. If you need a car, there are more ecothrifty options available now than ever before, from those that are commercially available to making your own. And if you own a car, there are things you can do to conserve resources and save money.

Electric vehicles

The availability of electric vehicles continues to increase and the prices continue to come down. They have zero emissions and are very quiet when driving because there is no engine. The capacity of the battery will be a factor in the price of the vehicle. The price goes up along with the size of the battery, which correlates with the distance the car can go on a single charge. If a car has only an electric motor, when it runs out of electricity, you will need a tow truck if you are not in a place where you can recharge the battery. Many people don't like this aspect of electric vehicles, although most people could drive back and forth to work on an electric battery because 50 percent of drivers commute less than ten miles to work every day, and 95 percent have a commute of less than forty miles.[47] An electric car can be recharged overnight, making it a good choice for a daily work commute.

There are also plug-in electric cars that have a gasoline engine. The car runs exclusively on electricity for shorter trips, and when the electricity

Do-it-yourself electric vehicles

Homemade electric vehicles are becoming more common. Although it may sound intimidating, the idea of building your own electric vehicle is gaining popularity. You can find a multitude of blogs and videos online about building your own bicycle, motorcycle, and car. Ben Nelson of Oconomowoc, Wisconsin, has built all three, even though he is not an engineer or a mechanic. In fact, he works in video production. He started with an electric powered bicycle, which he made from a kit in 2006 after seeing one at the Midwest Renewable Energy Association Fair in Wisconsin. He built an electric motorcycle in 2007, and in 2008, he built an electric car using an old Geo Metro. ☞

Ben's vehicles definitely fit the definition of ecothrifty, as he bought a used motorcycle and a used car and repurposed most parts. "The motorcycle project was almost exactly $2000 for the cycle, all the parts, and a motorcycle safety training class at my local college," he says. "When I started work on the car, I figured out a few ways to save on the cost of the project, including used batteries and a forklift motor. The entire car project cost me $1300." Buying a car that no longer has a working engine or exhaust system will save money on a do-it-yourself project because both are unnecessary and will be removed when converting the car to electric.

Of course, he had some challenges, but nothing that he couldn't overcome. "I had really never worked on cars before," Ben explains. "I was just working all by myself in my driveway, with basic tools. I had a lot of advice and support through the web forums, but sometimes I really just needed somebody else there to help show me the right way to do something. The challenge really never was complexity or any of the actual electric vehicle components. EVs are far simpler to work on than people think. Even the wiring is very easy. The hardest parts of these projects were things like dealing with rust, fixing brakes, and finding the right size bolts — just typical car repair challenges."

is depleted, the car switches over seamlessly to the gas engine. It has the benefit of using zero gasoline on shorter trips, but can be used for longer trips because of the gas engine.

Biodiesel

The original diesel engine was made to run on peanut oil. Petroleum-based diesel became the fuel of choice in the early twentieth century because it was abundant. It is possible, however, to use plant-based diesel in a diesel engine with no engine modifications. It is called biodiesel, and it is growing in popularity because it is biodegradable, non-toxic, and non-flammable. It can be made from any type of vegetable oil, although soybean oil is the most popular for commercially available biodiesel.

Some people have started to make their own biodiesel. Because it is illegal to sell biodiesel without performing lots of testing and being licensed, biodiesel cooperatives are gaining in popularity. Members of the biodiesel cooperative started by Steve Fugate of Iowa City pick up used fryer oil from restaurants and turn it into biodiesel, which they use in their vehicles. Over the past seven years, membership has varied from six to twelve people. Each member buys a share in the cooperative and then is entitled to purchase a percentage of the biodiesel that is created throughout the year. The price they pay per gallon basically covers the cost of production. Members who help produce the biodiesel pay less per gallon than do non-working members.

Members also have to pay a road use tax directly to the state of Iowa. Most drivers probably don't realize that in many states, part of the cost of commercial gasoline or diesel is a road use tax. Because they are not filling up at a gas station, each biodiesel co-op member has to keep track of how many gallons of biodiesel they use in their car, and pay the tax on that amount to the state.

In addition to saving members a considerable amount of money on their fuel bills, the biodiesel produced by Steve's co-op is especially eco-friendly because they use solar-thermal power and capture rainwater for use in the process of making the biodiesel.

The availability of used fryer oil varies from one place to another. In some areas, restaurants are happy to give it to you, according to Steve, because otherwise they have to pay to have it hauled away. In other areas, restaurants charge for it. If you are able to get used fryer oil free and you make your own biodiesel, you could save 40 to 50 percent on your fuel bill.

In 2006, a different type of biodiesel cooperative started in the Los Angeles area. Founders of the Biodiesel Cooperative of Los Angeles got together to purchase biodiesel in bulk for members. In addition to saving money, the group hoped to prove to retail fuel station operators that there was a demand for biodiesel in the LA area.

The co-op purchased a box cargo trailer for $13,000, which included three certified fuel storage containers with a simple pumping and metering system, and rented space in a private parking lot. Because they did not own land, they wanted the fueling station to be mobile so it could be moved easily from one location to another when necessary, or taken to an Earth Day event, school, or farmer's market for education purposes and membership recruitment.

The co-op expanded the number of fueling stations, each of which provides fuel for up to sixty members. The co-op is run entirely by volunteers, which includes a five-member governing board, trailer captains, a business manager, a few people who are handy with tools, and some who enjoy taking the trailers to events and chatting with the public. Members save 5 to 20 percent on the cost of fuel, even after paying their annual fee to the cooperative.[48]

Car care

Because the majority of people still drive cars powered by gasoline, it is important to know how to conserve fuel as much as possible. It may surprise you to learn how much you can save — or waste — by following a few simple guidelines.

Do

- Avoid jackrabbit starts, excessive braking, and speeding, which can decrease fuel efficiency by up to 33 percent.
- Drive sixty miles per hour or less. Every five miles per hour that you drive in excess of sixty miles per hour is the equivalent of paying 7 percent more per gallon of gas. For example, if gas is $4 a gallon, and you are driving seventy miles per hour, it is like paying 46 cents more per gallon of gas than if you were driving sixty miles per hour.[49]
- Follow the manufacturer's recommendations for scheduled maintenance.
- Check your owner's manual to see how often you should have the oil changed. There was a time when all cars were supposed to have their oil changed every 3,000 miles, but manufacturers of most vehicles made in the twenty-first century recommend less frequent oil changes. While many suggest an oil change somewhere between 5,000 and 10,000 miles, some carmakers say you can go as long as 15,000 miles between oil changes. Doing it more often is a waste of money and oil.

- Inflate the car's tires to the level recommended by the manufacturer. Not only does it increase the life of the tires, it also saves gasoline.
- Use the octane level recommended by your car's manufacturer. Using a higher grade of gasoline will not result in better gas mileage or longer engine life. The only reason to switch to a higher grade of gasoline is if your car consistently makes a knocking or pinging sound when using the grade of gasoline recommended by the manufacturer.[50]

Don't

- Don't start your car and let it idle for more than thirty seconds before driving. Your car will actually warm up faster once you're driving, and it is better for the engine than idling because the engine is not operating at peak temperature when idling. A car idling for two minutes uses as much gas as driving one mile.[51]
- Don't leave heavy things in your car because it reduces your gas mileage by as much as 2 percent for each additional one hundred pounds of stuff.
- Don't use a luggage rack on top of your car. It creates drag and can reduce fuel efficiency by 5 percent.[52]

New or used

If you are not up for making your own electric vehicle but you need a car, you are probably wondering if you should buy new or used. Twenty years ago, it was always a better idea to buy new because used cars were just big bundles of repair bills waiting to happen. However, cars have become far more reliable in the last couple decades. It is one instance where the axiom "They don't make 'em like they used to!" is a good thing. It is not unusual today for cars to go more than 200,000 miles. However, there are a few caveats. Obviously, not all used cars are equally reliable.

One big variable is the care that the car received from its previous owner. If the car was properly maintained, it will ultimately have a longer useful life than if oil changes and other routine maintenance operations were ignored. When buying a used car, look for one previously owned by someone who kept records of regular maintenance.

It is usually most cost effective to keep a car for many years, rather than to trade it in for a new one every few years. If the car needs a big repair, divide the cost by twelve to see how it would compare to a monthly car payment if you bought a new car. Although $1,200 sounds like an expensive repair, it comes out to only $100 a month, which is far less than a loan payment on a new or gently used car.

CHAPTER 10

Free or Practically Free

While it is true in many cases that "you get what you pay for," meaning cheap price usually equals cheap quality, it is also true that there are some great things to be had for no money at all.

Bartering

Before we moved to the country, I never thought about bartering, probably because I didn't think I had anything to trade. My first barter involved livestock. I had too many turkey gobblers, so I traded a breeding pair of turkeys to someone for a sheep that she didn't need. After a few more trades, I realized that everyone, whether they live in the city or the country, has goods and services to barter.

Babysitting co-ops are essentially barter exchanges. Each co-op member has an account that tracks hours used and hours worked. Rather than trading babysitting with one specific person, in a co-op you accumulate credits by babysitting other members' children, and you spend those credits buying babysitting services from other members for your children. It doesn't matter whether you ever babysit for the person who babysat your children. For example, if you babysit for three different people for a total of twelve hours, the co-op now owes you twelve hours of babysitting, which can be provided by any of the members.

When my children were small, I knew two women who helped each other clean their houses. Not only did this save money compared with hiring a cleaning service, it also made housecleaning a social activity rather than a boring chore, and their children could play together. By consolidating the cleaning with a play date, they were also saving the gasoline a hired cleaner would have used when driving to the house to clean it.

Gardeners can trade produce, flowers, and herbs with friends who garden. It is a rare year when everything in your garden grows perfectly, so if your zucchini was attacked by squash bugs, you might be able to get zucchini from a friend by trading for something that grew well in your garden. It is unlikely that you yourself will use all of the apples or pears that mature fruit trees produce, so you can trade some of them with a friend who has something else. If you don't like to garden but you enjoy baking bread, perhaps you can trade bread for garden produce with a gardening friend. Don't have a yard? You could help a gardening friend or a farmer with the garden work in exchange for some of the harvest. On the flip side, if you have space for a garden but don't know a trowel from a tiller, you could let a gardening friend plant a garden in your yard and share the bounty.

A meal co-op with a neighbor (or two) who shares your food and meal preferences provides an alternative to takeout or eating out. Once a week you double (or triple) the meal you are cooking, and the other family gets dinner prepared for them. On another night, they fix dinner for you. Your neighbors can eat at your house or pick up the dinner and dine at home. Because with many recipes it takes no more time (or electricity or natural gas) to double or triple a recipe, this practice requires you to invest no additional time on the night you fix dinner, and you save time on the nights the other members of the co-op fix dinner for you. You still get home-cooked meals, which are more likely to be free of preservatives and artificial ingredients, and you save money on the gasoline used driving to and from a restaurant. Your electric or gas bill will also probably be lower because it takes no more power to bake two or three loaves of bread (or casseroles) than it does to bake one.

At one time, bartering was only done between people who knew each other or met each other through a notice posted on a community bulletin board at the supermarket or post office, but today it is possible to barter via the Internet. People can use Craigslist and Facebook to set up trades with strangers and friends alike, and there are even online sites set up specifically for bartering so that you can trade goods and services with people you don't know and who may not even have something you want. Users post what they want and what they have to trade, and although one-on-one trades can happen, there can also be multiuser trades. For example, John wants Rachel's car, but Rachel does not want John's boat. No problem, because Rachel wants several things listed by Miguel. The computer system keeps track of all the trading and the values of items. It also helps match up people who have things for barter with people who are looking for those items. When doing long-distance trades, you may not know exactly what you are receiving, but this also happens with buying on any site online. The bartering sites operate like eBay and other online sites where real money changes hands. There are buyer and seller reviews, and the host will sanction users who don't adhere to the terms of service.

> **Savings:** Depending on how much you barter, you could save anywhere from a few dollars to thousands of dollars per year. A dinner co-op could save a family of four anywhere from $1,040 ($20 per meal) to $2,600 ($50 per meal) every year by reducing eating out by one meal a week. A babysitting co-op could save you $1,000 a year if you eliminate hiring a babysitter once a week for two hours at $10 an hour or for three hours a week at $7 an hour.

Learning

I was an early adopter of the Internet. Back in 1993, I frequented online bulletin boards, learning how to train my dog from professional dog trainers and how to care for my daughter's guinea pig from guinea pig breeders.

The technology of the Internet has evolved tremendously since then, offering a variety of platforms for meeting others and discussing common interests. There are groups, forums, blogs, and social networks online. Groups are available for people with every imaginable hobby, occupation, medical condition, and lifestyle. After joining, you can post questions, and you can receive responses from the members. You can go to the group site online to read messages, or you can sign up to have messages sent to your inbox as email.

Online groups get a lot of credit for my learning to homestead after moving to the country from the Chicago suburbs. I joined groups on raising chickens, pigs, cattle, goats, sheep, and turkeys, as well as on gardening, cheese making, soap making, and homesteading.

Some people don't like the single list of posts in Yahoo! and Google, and if you find it difficult to keep track of questions and answers on those sites, you might enjoy forums more. Forums are set up with a list of categories and subcategories on the home page, and you post your question in the appropriate subcategory. Although this system makes it easier to read only the categories that interest you, it also makes it easier to miss a post because you have to look at multiple lists rather than only one.

In recent years, a new hybrid of Internet communication has opened up — communities and social networks where people can create their own pages with a forum, photo albums, videos, and a blog, such as Ning and Big Tent. Many of these groups even have chat rooms available for instant communication.

You can get a lot of free advice by using the Internet, and you can read about situations that you might never learn about otherwise because there is such a diverse range of people sharing experiences. It can be tough sometimes to weed out the good advice from the not-so-good advice online. Groups and forums have an advantage over websites and blogs that if someone gives advice that is completely off base, another group member will likely disagree and offer you their suggestion for your situation. Although this can create conflict, most groups have rules about how members are expected to communicate. Some have strict rules against "flaming," while others allow members to express

> **Savings:** If you are able to cancel a magazine subscription and avoid buying a couple of books to learn about a subject, you can easily save $50. Subtract a conference and you've saved several hundred dollars after registration fees, hotel, and travel expenses. Although you should not substitute group membership for sound medical advice, some people have avoided vet bills by learning what is "normal" animal behavior from Internet group members. For example, our English shepherd once had an episode of reverse sneezing, which looks and sounds scary but does not hurt a dog. After I described on an Internet group what he did, several people immediately said it sounded like reverse sneezing, and I was able to avoid an after-hours emergency trip to the vet, which would have been a minimum of $75.

themselves freely and without concern for misinterpretation. The good news is that there are so many groups available you can find one with etiquette rules that are comfortable for you. Like groups in the real world, some are friendlier than others.

Using Internet groups, forums, and communities, as well as social networking, can save money and trees by reducing the number of books and magazines you might otherwise purchase for education on a specific topic. By providing access to experts and mentors, Internet groups can save fuel otherwise used travelling to a class or conference on a specific topic.

Repurposing and reusing

One person's trash is another person's treasure. This is the basis of Freecycle, an online community where everything is free. As a member of an online group in your area, you can post items for giveaway that you no longer want, and alternatively you can acquire items that others have posted for giveaway. If you need something in particular, you don't have to wait until someone posts it. You can post a request for specific items. People on both sides of the transaction work to keep items from the landfill. There are almost five thousand groups with more than eight million members worldwide. Groups can be found at freecycle.org.

Yes, some people (like us) have given away an ugly 1950s-era dresser with broken handles, but there are creative people out there who love the idea of stripping and painting old furniture and putting on new handles to create a cool, "new" dresser. There are also plenty of things listed that can be used without refurbishing, such as two-thirds of a box of new shingles, which could be used to roof a child's playhouse or a potting shed. I have a friend who picked up a "new" area rug for her family room.

Freecycle can help you de-clutter your house. You may not have thought anyone would want your ugly (fill in the blank), but someone probably does. I was ecstatic when I saw someone giving away the twenty-volume, 1973 *Better Homes and Gardens Encyclopedia of Cooking* because I collect old cookbooks. If your stuff has outgrown your house and garage and you are one of the millions of people who rent storage space elsewhere, you definitely need to become acquainted with Freecycle. Have a yard sale first, if you feel you must get some money back from all of your clutter, but when the sale is over, start posting on Freecycle.

There are also listings for free items on Craigslist, and many people are now posting things they want to give away on their Facebook page. I have a friend who recently picked up a free hot tub that another friend posted on Facebook.

Even if something can be recycled in the traditional sense, it is often recycled into something of inferior quality, whereas you might be able to upcycle an item — create a new item that is superior to the original. I have seen a number of beautiful greenhouses online that were made from old windows, men's shirts that were made into pillows, a wine bottle turned into a tiki torch, and an old sweater that was turned into a pet bed. Of course, traditional recycling is better than sending things to a landfill, but repurposing an item is even better.

Foraging

Searching for food might sound like something one can do only in the wilderness, but people are starting to forage in cities. Alexandra

Free Stuff Online

There are a lot of websites online that claim to offer free stuff. However, we all know there is no such thing as a free lunch. Many of the things given away are small samples of processed food products, and the goal of free samples is to create a long-term customer. It is less expensive to make the product yourself than to pay for prepared foods, and your time will be rewarded in savings, and it might not turn out to save you anything over the cost of homemade if you have to pay for shipping. Samples, like single servings, are not ecofriendly, producing a lot of packaging that winds up in a landfill. While there might be some legitimate freebies out there, the time it takes to find them could be better invested.

Gomez-Koski of Chicago began foraging for pumpkins in 2010 somewhat serendipitously.

"A few days after Halloween, I was scrolling through the free section on Craigslist when I found a post offering leftover, uncut pumpkins," Alexandra explained. "So I went and picked up a few pumpkins from the original Craigslist poster, and then I went kind of pumpkin crazy. I figured if a few pumpkins were good, a lot were even better. So when I was walking around after Halloween and I would see uncarved pumpkins in front of houses, I rang their doorbell and asked if they still wanted them. Some people looked at me like I was crazy, but most people were happy to get rid of their pumpkins. Eventually, I ended up with around twenty pumpkins of all different sizes."

She then used the pumpkins to make all sorts of sweet and savory dishes. "I made pumpkin pies, pumpkin cheesecakes, breads, muffins, soups and curries," she said. "We ate mashed pumpkin either sweetened with a bit of sugar and coconut milk or made savory with butter, salt, and pepper." She also pureed cooked pumpkin and froze it for adding to oatmeal or fruit smoothies, and she roasted the seeds for snacking.

If you decide to forage in an urban environment, it is important to make sure you are not doing anything illegal. Whether the food is on public or private property, ask for permission to remove it. Otherwise, you could find yourself in trouble like a lot of people in New York City's parks did in 2011. Park rangers had to start cracking down on people who were taking large quantities of wild fruits and herbs, as well as taking fish and turtles. One can be fined as much as $250 for removing plants from the city's parks in New York. In other public areas, such as Sandy Hook in New Jersey, foragers are limited to one quart per person per day.[53]

You may assume that a plant is abundant and growing wild in an area, but this may not always be the case. For example, the non-profit Central Park Conservancy works to reintroduce species such as wild ginger that have died out or were illegally removed by foragers in Central Park.[54]

Final Thoughts

The biggest hurdle in accomplishing any of the projects in this book is planning and organization. Nothing in this book is particularly difficult, but the hardest part of any project is simply getting started. It is so easy to keep saying that you want to do something — someday. So, right now, before you put down this book, flip back through it and pick out three things that you really will do. Choose one thing that you can do today — like using baking soda as a facial scrub. Choose one that you can accomplish this week — like making something from scratch that you have been buying ready-made. And choose one that will require you to make some plans, such as buying half a cow directly from a farmer or hosting a clothing swap.

If you don't have a planning calendar, find one on your computer or online. Most computers and many email programs have calendars that you can use to break down your goals into small chunks and post them on your target completion dates. You can also set up the calendar to send you email reminders to keep you on track. For example, if you want to host a clothing swap, make a list of everything you need to do to make it happen, and then put those things on your calendar — pick a date, establish guidelines for the swap, invite friends and email guidelines, plan food and drink, borrow clothing racks or folding tables, and so on. Set it up so that it will automatically send you an email or a text message to remind you to accomplish each step of your goal on time.

Accept your limitations. We avoided learning to make wine for years because we wanted to use our own grapes, and we were having a terrible time keeping grape vines alive. Finally, I realized that by making wine from concentrated grape juice, we could still learn most of the principles of wine making, save a lot of money on buying wine, and keep a lot of wine bottles out of the recycling facilities. Even if you can't do everything that you want to do, start somewhere. Doing a little is better than doing nothing.

Everyone that I interviewed for this book advised novices to just jump right in and get started with whatever project. Mistakes are inevitable, but don't let them slow you down. Learn from them and move on. And if you make the same mistake again, don't beat yourself up. My biggest challenge in gardening was simply remembering to water and weed! But we eventually got it right, and you can, too. With a little practice, patience, and persistence, you can make cheaper, greener choices for a happier, healthier life.

Bibliography

American Academy of Pediatrics. "Baby Walkers: A Dangerous Choice." HealthyChildren.org, 2012. healthychildren.org/English/safety-preven tion/at-home/pages/Baby-Walkers-A-Dangerous-Choice.aspx.

Birt, D.F. "Update on the Effects of Vitamins A, C, and E and Selenium on Carcinogenesis." Abstract. 183(3):311-20 of *Proceedings of the Society for Experimental Biology and Medicine*. Society for Experimental Biology and Medicine. New York: December 1986. ncbi.nlm.nih.gov/pubmed/354 0970.

Bruce, Debra. "Chronic Constipation: Facts vs. Myths." WebMD, June 20, 2007. webmd.com/digestive-disorders/features/chronic-constipation-facts-vs -myths.

Butterfield, Bruce. "The Impact of Home and Community Gardening in America." National Gardening Association, 2009. gardenresearch.com /files/2009-Impact-of-Gardening-in-America-White-Paper.pdf.

California Energy Commission. "Clothes Dryers." California Energy Commission; Consumer Energy Center, 2012. consumerenergy center.org /home/appliances/dryers.html.

———. "Should I Shut Off the Motor When I'm Idling My Car?" California Energy Commission; Consumer Energy Center, 2012. consumerenergy center.org/myths/idling.html.

————. "Urban Myth: Leaving a Fluorescent Light On Is Cheaper than Turning It Off and On." California Energy Commission; Consumer Energy Center, 2012. consumerenergycenter.org/myths/fluorescent_lights .html.

Can Manufacturers Institute. "The Can: A Sustainable Solution." Can Manufacturers Institute, 2006. cancentral.com/sustainability/solution-1.cfm.

————. "Recycling Fun Facts." Can Manufacturers Institute, 2006. cancen tral.com/funFacts.cfm.

Centers for Disease Control and Prevention. "Americans Make Nearly Four Medical Visits a Year On Average." Centers for Disease Control and Prevention; NCHS Press Room, August 6, 2008. cdc.gov/nchs/pressroom /08newsreleases/visitstodoctor.htm.

————. "Ambulatory Care Use and Physician Visits." Centers for Disease Control and Prevention; FastStats, December 12, 2011. cdc.gov/nchs /fastats/docvisit.htm.

Chua, Jasmin Malik. "Beat the Heat, Wash in Cold." Planet Green (blog). HowStuffWorks.com, January 11, 2012. tlc.howstuffworks.com/home /beat-the-heat-wash-in-cold.htm.

Consumers Union. "Consumer Reports: Genetically Modified Foods in Your Shopping Cart." News release. Consumers Union, August 23, 1999. consumersunion.org/food/gefny999.htm.

————. "6 Big Ways to Save on Infant Formula." ConsumerReports.org; Consumer News, March 3, 2008. news.consumerreports.org/baby/2008 /03/6-big-ways-to-s.html

————. "Cloth vs. Disposable Diapers: Getting Started." ConsumerReports. org; Consumer News, July 8, 2009. news.consumerreports.org/baby /2009/07/cloth-vs-disposable-diapers-getting-started.html.

————. "Is Tap Water Safer Than Bottled?" ConsumerReports.org; Consumer News, July 10, 2009. news.consumerreports.org/safety/2009/07 /is-tap-water-safer-than-bottled-water.html.

Container Recycling Institute. "PET Recycling vs. Utilization Rates." Container Recycling Institute. container-recycling.org/facts/plastic/data /petrecutil.htm.

Energy Star. "How Much Water Do Energy Star Dishwashers Use?" Energy Star, last modified April 28, 2011. energystar.supportportal.com/ics /support/kbAnswer.asp?deptID=23018&task=knowledge&question ID=17719.

Environmental Working Group. "Sugar in Children's Cereals." Environmental Working Group, December 2011. ewg.org/report/sugar_in_childrens _cereals/more_sugar.

———. "EWG's Skin Deep Cosmetic's Database." Environmental Working Group, 2012. ewg.org/skindeep/.

Fitzgerald, Garrett and Rob van Haaren. "How Far Do We Drive and Can EVs Satisfy Our Needs? Solar Journey USA, 2012. solarjourneyusa.com /EVdistanceAnalysis.php.

Foderaro, Lisa W. "Enjoy Park Greenery, City Says, But Not as Salad." *New York Times* online, July 29, 2011. nytimes.com/2011/07/30/nyregion /new-york-moves-to-stop-foraging-in-citys-parks.html.

Ginsberg, David, Sidney Phillips, Joyce Wallace, and Karen Josephson. "Evaluating and Managing Constipation in the Elderly: Costs." Medscape Today, June 2007. medscape.com/viewarticle/559895_4.

Harvard School of Public Health. "Consuming Canned Soup Linked to Greatly Elevated Levels of the Chemical BPA." News release, November, 22, 2011. hsph.harvard.edu/news/press-releases/2011-releases/canned -soup-bpa.html.

Layton, Lyndsey and Christopher Lee. "Canada Bans BPA From Baby Bottles." *Washington Post* online, April 19, 2008. washingtonpost.com/wp -dyn/content/article/2008/04/18/AR2008041803036.html.

Lunder, Sonya and Jane Houlihan. "EWG's Guide to Infant Formula and Baby Bottles." Environmental Working Group, December 2007. ewg.org /reports/infantformula.

Madison Gas and Electric. "Home Equipment Cost of Operation." Madison Gas and Electric; Appliances and Equipment. mge.com/home/appliances /cost.htm.

Mancino, Lisa and Jean Buzby. "Americans' Whole-Grain Consumption Below Guidelines." *Amber Waves,* April 2005. ers.usda.gov/amberwaves /april05/findings/WholeGrainConsumption.htm.

Marketplace Staff. "The Cost of the Common Cold." Marketplace Money, January 21, 2011. marketplace.org/topics/life/cost-common-cold.

Markets and Markets. "Global Baby Food Market 2009–2014."Markets and Markets, July 2009. marketsandmarkets.com/Market-Reports/baby -food-global-market-75.html.

McDonough, Pat, with Chad Dreas and Zach Kennedy. "As US Screens Grow, So Does U.S. DVR Usage," *Neilsen Wire,* February 29, 2012. blog

.nielsen.com/nielsenwire/media_entertainment/as-tv-screens-grow-so
-does-u-s-dvr-usage/.

Naidenko, Olga, Nneka Leiba, Renee Sharp, and Jane Houlihan. "Bottled
Water Quality Investigation: 10 Major Brands, 38 Pollutants." Environ-
mental Working Group, October 2008. ewg.org/reports/BottledWater
/Bottled-Water-Quality-Investigation.

Natural Resources Defense Council. "Bottled Water." Natural Resources Defense Council, last revised April 25, 2008. nrdc.org/water/drinking/qbw
.asp.

Nielsen. "What Consumers Watch: Nielsen's Q1 2010 Three Screen Report."
Neilsen Wire, June 11, 2010. blog.nielsen.com/nielsenwire/online_mo
bile/what-consumers-watch-nielsens-q1-2010-three-sscreen-report/.

Niemann, Deborah. *Homegrown and Handmade: A Practical Guide to More
Self-Reliant Living.* Gabriola Island, BC: New Society Publishers, 2011.

Peterson, Josh. "Switch Off These 8 Commonly Left-On Appliances." Planet
Green (blog), HowStuffWorks.com, January 11, 2012. tlc.howstuffworks
.com/home/commonly-lefton-appliances.htm.

Pollan, Michael. "Out of the Kitchen, Onto the Couch." *New York Times*
online, July 29, 2009. nytimes.com/2009/08/02/magazine/02cooking-t
.html?pagewanted=all.

PRWeb. "Global Market for Feminine Hygiene Products to Reach US$14.3
Billion by 2015, According to New Report by Global Industry Analysts,
Inc." News release. PRWeb, January 6, 2011. prweb.com/releases/2011/1
/prweb8046503.htm.

Rodgers, Lisa. "The Cosmetic Ingredient Review and Safe Cosmetics." Personal Care (blog), August 5, 2011. personalcaretruth.com/2011/08/the
-cosmetic-ingredient-review-and-safe-cosmetics/.

Slone Epidemiology Center. "Patterns of Medication Use in the United States
2006." Slone Survey, last revised April 26, 2011. bu.edu/slone/Slone
Survey/AnnualRpt/SloneSurveyWebReport2006.pdf.

US Bureau of Labor Statistics. "100 Years of U.S. Consumer Spending: Data
for the Nation, New York City, and Boston." US Bureau of Labor Statistics, last revised August 3, 2006. bls.gov/opub/uscs/.

———. "American Time Use Survey Summary." News release. US Bureau of
Labor Statistics, June 22, 2011. bls.gov/news.release/atus.nr0.htm.

US Department of Energy. "Driving More Efficiently." US Department of Energy; fueleconomy.gov, last modified May 21, 2012. fueleconomy.gov /feg/driveHabits.shtml.

———. "How Energy Efficient Light Bulbs Compare With Traditional Incandescents." US Department of Energy; Energy Savers, last revised May 21, 2012. energysavers.gov/your_home/lighting_daylighting/index.cfm /mytopic=12060.

US Federal Trade Commission, "The Low-Down on High Octane Gasoline." US Federal Trade Commission; Facts for Consumers, last revised April 24, 2009. ftc.gov/bcp/edu/pubs/consumer/autos/aut12.shtm.

———. "Saving Money at the Pump: Tips to Stretch Your Gas Dollars." US Federal Trade Commission; FTC Alert, last revised May 25 2011. ftc.gov /bcp/edu/pubs/consumer/alerts/alt064.shtm.

US Food and Drug Administration. "Guide to Inspections of Cosmetic Product Manufacturers." US Food and Drug Administration, last revised March 13, 2009. fda.gov/ICECI/Inspections/InspectionGuides/ucm 074952.htm.

van Poppel, Geert and Henk van den Berg. "Vitamins and Cancer." Abstract. *Cancer Letters* 114, no. 1-2 (1997): 195–202. ncbi.nlm.nih.gov/pubmed /9103291.

Walsh, Bryan. "The Perils of Plastic." *Time* (online), April 1, 2010. time.com /time/specials/packages/article/0,28804,1976909_1976908_19769 38,00.html.

Notes

1 US Bureau of Labor Statistics, "American Time Use Survey Summary."
2 Pat McDonough, Chad Dreas, and Zach Kennedy, "As U.S. Screens Grow, So Does U.S. DVR Usage."
3 US Bureau of Labor Statistics, "100 Years of U.S. Consumer Spending."
4 D. Niemann, *Homegrown and Handmade.*
5 Lisa Rodgers, "The Cosmetic Ingredient Review and Safe Cosmetics."
6 US Food and Drug Administration, "Guide to Inspections of Cosmetic Product Manufacturers."
7 Environmental Working Group, "EWG's Skin Deep Cosmetic's Database."
8 PRWeb, "Global Market for Feminine Hygiene Products."
9 Centers for Disease Control and Prevention, "Ambulatory Care Use and Physician Visits."
10 Centers for Disease Control and Prevention, "Americans Make Nearly Four Medical Visits a Year on Average."
11 Slone Epidemiology Center, 2006, "Patterns of Medication Use in the United States," 22.
12 Marketplace Staff, "The Cost of the Common Cold."
13 Debra Bruce, "Chronic Constipation."
14 David Ginsberg et al., "Evaluating and Managing Constipation in the Elderly: Costs."
15 Lisa Mancino and Jean Buzby, "Americans' Whole-Grain Consumption

Below Guidelines."

16 D.F. Birt, "Update on the Effects of Vitamins A, C, and E and Selenium on Carcinogenesis."

17 Geert van Poppel and Henk van den Berg, "Cancer and Vitamins."

18 Consumers Union, "Consumer Reports: Genetically Modified Foods in Your Shopping Cart."

19 Lyndsey Layton and Christopher Lee, "Canada Bans BPA from Baby Bottles."

20 Sonya Lunder and Jane Houlihan, "EWG's Guide to Infant Formula and Baby Bottles."

21 Consumers Union, "6 big ways to save on infant formula."

22 Consumers Union, "Cloth vs. disposable diapers: Getting started."

23 Markets and Markets, "Global Baby Food Market 2009–2014," under "Summary."

24 American Academy of Pediatrics, "Baby Walkers: A Dangerous Choice."

25 US Bureau of Labor Statistics, "Consumer Expenditures and Income."

26 Harvard School of Public Health, "Consuming Canned Soup Linked to Greatly Elevated Levels of the Chemical BPA."

27 Michael Pollan, "Out of the Kitchen, Onto the Couch."

28 Environmental Working Group, "Sugar in Children's Cereals."

29 Consumers Union, "Is tap water safer than bottled?

30 Olga Naidenko, "Bottled Water Quality Investigation: 10 Major Brands, 38 Pollutants."

31 Consumers Union, "Is tap water safer than bottled?"

32 Natural Resources Defense Council, "Bottled Water."

33 Container Recycling Institute. "PET Recycling vs. Utilization Rates."

34 Can Manufacturers Institute, "Recycling Fun Facts."

35 Ibid., "The Can: A Sustainable Solution."

36 Madison Gas and Electric, "Home Equipment Cost of Operation."

37 Josh Peterson, "Switch Off These 8 Commonly Left-On Appliances."

38 Energy Star, "How Much Water Do Energy Star Dishwashers Use?"

39 Energy Star appliance label.

40 Jasmin Malik Chua, "Beat the Heat, Wash in Cold."

41 California Energy Commission, "Clothes Dryers."

42 US Department of Energy, "How Energy-Efficient Light Bulbs Compare with Traditional Incandescents."

43 California Energy Commission, "Urban Myth."

44 Ibid.

45 Bruce Butterfield, "The Impact of Home and Community Gardening in America."

46 Nielsen, "What Consumers Watch: Nielsen's Q1 2010 Three Screen Report."

47 Garrett Fitzgerald and Rob van Haaren, "How far do we drive and can EVs satisfy our needs?"

48 Biodiesel Cooperative of Los Angeles, members of the board of directors, personal communication with the author, April 2, 2012.

49 US Department of Energy, "Driving More Efficiently," under "Observe the Speed Limit."

50 US Federal Trade Commission, "The Low-Down on High Octane Gasoline."

51 California Energy Commission, "Should I Shut Off the Motor When I'm Idling My Car?"

52 US Federal Trade Commission, "Saving Money at the Pump: Tips to Stretch Your Gas Dollars."

53 Lisa Foderaro, "Enjoy Park Greenery."

54 Scott Johnson (former Director of Communication and Branding, Central Park Conservancy), personal communication with the author, November 7, 2011.

Recipe Index

Index

About the Author

Deborah Niemann is a homesteader, writer and self-sufficiency expert. In 2002, she relocated her family from the suburbs of Chicago to a 32 acre parcel on a creek "in the middle of nowhere". Together, they built their own home and began growing the majority of their own food. Sheep, pigs, cattle, goats, chickens, and turkeys supply meat, eggs and dairy products, while an organic garden and orchard provides fruit and vegetables. A highly sought-after speaker and workshop leader, Deborah presents extensively on topics including soapmaking, breadbaking, cheesemaking, composting and homeschooling. She is also the author of *Homegrown & Handmade.*

If you have enjoyed *Ecothrifty*, you might also enjoy other

BOOKS TO BUILD A NEW SOCIETY

Our books provide positive solutions for people who
want to make a difference. We specialize in:

**Sustainable Living • Green Building • Peak Oil
Renewable Energy • Environment & Economy
Natural Building & Appropriate Technology
Progressive Leadership • Resistance and Community
Educational & Parenting Resources**

New Society Publishers

ENVIRONMENTAL BENEFITS STATEMENT

New Society Publishers has chosen to produce this book on recycled paper made
with **100% post consumer waste,** processed chlorine free, and old growth free.

For every 5,000 books printed, New Society saves the following resources:[1]

9	Trees
815	Pounds of Solid Waste
897	Gallons of Water
1,170	Kilowatt Hours of Electricity
1,482	Pounds of Greenhouse Gases
6	Pounds of HAPs, VOCs, and AOX Combined
2	Cubic Yards of Landfill Space

[1]Environmental benefits are calculated based on research done by the Environmental Defense Fund
and other members of the Paper Task Force who study the environmental impacts of the paper
industry.

For a full list of NSP's titles, please call 1-800-567-6772 *or check out our website* at:

www.newsociety.com